Seven Steps To Hell and Back

The story of a combat veteran, a "Death Wish" Journey, and how he struggled to adapt to a civilian world.

"Not All Wounds Are Visible"

GERMANY

SEVEN STEPS

FRANK E. WIGGINS
written with
Etta Cavalier

What Others Are Saying

Reading "Seven Steps to Hell" reinforces my belief in how inhumane we as the human race can be; yet miraculously at the same time, we are somehow able to overcome those very obstacles the inhumanity continually perpetuates. Mr. Wiggins' story is a true example of this. I must comment it is not pleasant to read the horrible experiences Mr. Wiggins endured; however, his personal triumph of sharing his story will no doubt help other service men and women who have experienced similar events in their lives. Not only did Mr. Wiggins dutifully endure what he felt was required of him as an enlisted service man serving his country, unfortunately he also came back to an American society who did not understand what he had gone through nor does it appear he received appropriate recognition proportionate to the difficulty of his tours. Despite this, he remains steadfast about what he knows and believes is his duty now, which is to share his incredible story to the rest of the world.

The horrors Mr. Wiggins experienced will never leave him; however, remarkably over time he has been able to deaden to a lesser degree the stinging psychological pain of his experiences and move onward with support from his close friends and family. His resolve and determination is now to speak openly about his military ordeal with the sole intent of helping others to heal.

I have worked extensively as a Pain Management Clinical Pharmacy Specialist at the New Mexico VA Health Care System treating chronic pain patients who have a concurrent diagnosis of Post Traumatic Stress Disorder (PTSD). From my own understanding of what negative impact PTSD can have on the personal lives of those who suffer from this diagnosis, I know for a fact, that for Mr. Wiggins to reach the level of trust necessary to write about his personal military trauma is a huge mile stone for him and an incredible benefit to those who will read his personal account. Being able to put into writing his story so that others may learn and reflect on their own personal life experiences is Mr. Wiggins' gift to the world and reading this book is highly recommended to all, regardless of whether or not you served in the armed forces.

P. David Pacheco, R.Ph., Ph.C., PA-C, CAAAPM
Clinical Pharmacy Specialist
Formulary Drug Policy Manager
New Mexico VA Health Care System
Albuquerque, New Mexico 87108

Frank Wiggins has done an excellent job of describing PTSD and what it can do to a person! After reading this book, I feel as if I know him. His conversations with his son lead us into the family system where PTSD is held, opening up the 'cocoon'. Stunning! It really brings it home to all of us. No more secrets and shame that hold the "IT" of PTSD in place.

Well done! I plan to use this with Veteran couples as they show up to finally be free of their trauma brought on by war.

Much love and respect,

Candace Green, Program Director
National Veteran Wellness and Healing Retreats,
Cardinal Retreats

At the age of 18, Frank Wiggins entered the U.S. Army in 1959 and was trained to clear minefields in Germany's buffer zone with Russia. By the age of 20, Frank was a war veteran and expert survivor, torn with memories, nightmares and unbelievable amounts of suppressed stress and rage. And yet, this is an amazing story of courage and resiliency in the aftermath of years of flashbacks and unresolved trauma, now known as Post Traumatic Stress Disorder, or PTSD.

We have few first-hand reports with the level of detail that Frank is able to recall. Two (of many) important comments he makes, "That's been with me for a long, long time." And "I was nineteen when I left for that seventh mission and that's where I stayed stuck in my mind. I'm going to be seventy years old, and to this day, I still don't feel like I've reached twenty." sums up his experiences greater than anything I could write.

I am deeply touched by Frank's story, and I think that many others will find his journey, rough and dangerous as it was, to ultimately be about hope and recovery. Unresolved wounds and traumas, especially those experienced by our veterans, keep many from experiencing full and happy lives. Diagnosed with PTSD in 1995 and denied VA benefits, living with a Death Wish and through years of feeling No Fear, Frank has survived on wits and strength that most of us can't even (or don't want to) imagine.

While Frank's story makes my heart ache and my tears run, his courage and clarity give us all hope. Frank's courage in telling his story has led him to find greater peace and healing; I pray that more veterans find their way, find their voice, and once again know peace.

Celia Hildebrand, M.S., LAc, Dipl Oriental Medicine
(NCCAOM) Volunteer at Acupuncturists Without Borders / Military
Stress Reduction Project

SEVEN STEPS TO HELL AND BACK
"Not All Wounds Are Visible"

FRANK E. WIGGINS

Written with
Etta Cavalier

The Story of a Combat Veteran, a "Death Wish" Journey, and how he struggled to adapt to a civilian world.

SEVEN STEPS TO HELL AND BACK

Published by
F.E.W. Stories Publications
Albuquerque, New Mexico

Wiggins, Frank E. & Cavalier, Etta
Seven Steps to Hell and Back: Not all wounds are visible/
Wiggins, Frank E. & Cavalier, Etta

ISBN: 978-0-615-23181-5
Library of Congress Control Number: 2011934534

Manufactured in the United State of America

This book is dedicated

to all my fellow veterans

who have gone through

similar experiences.

CONTENTS

DISCLAIMER

Certain names, characters and incidents portrayed herein have been changed for purposes of this book, and any similarity to the names, characters, or history of any actual persons living or dead other than Frank E. Wiggins is entirely coincidental and unintentional.

ACKNOWLEDGEMENTS

To my wife Lenora and children; Vivian, Frank Jr, Louie, Willie, Ray and Jaime, who with Love and perseverance, have stood by me throughout my turbulent years, and to my grandchildren whom I love so dearly; Carla, April, James, Lester, Moses, Linkin, and not to forget, my two adorable great grand daughters, Alexa and Denelle.

To Matthew and Sheri Cox for their support and expertise in helping publish this book.

I especially want to express my thanks and gratitude to Etta Cavalier, who volunteered to take on this big endeavor. This book would not have been possible without the countless hours Etta has dedicated to the writing and editing of this project. And to my brother, Andy Cavalier, thank you for all your support throughout the years.

Foreword

I first met Frank Wiggins through a mutual veteran friend in 2000, and over the ensuing years, I have gotten to know him well. I have also become keenly aware first hand of the common symptoms associated with Post Traumatic Stress Disorder, (PTSD) of which many veterans have been diagnosed with.

The collaboration of this book between Frank and I began three years ago when I volunteered to be his "back-up" author. Ray, his son, recorded hours of conversations with his father, and I helped Ray transfer these digital recordings into audio CD's. Frank had solicited the assistance of a relative to transcribe and edit the material, but in the end, that did not materialize.

Several months earlier, I had told him, "Frank, if this fails again and you can't find anyone to help you write your book, I'll be your last resort." I did this with sincere intentions. I was not a professional writer, but was convinced that his story needed to be told. I have been a counselor and educator for over thirty-five years. During the last ten years, I have had the privilege of meeting veterans who served during the Cold War, Korean War, Vietnam, Desert Storm, Iraq, Afghanistan and others, who can't remember or say where they have been. They know they have been in combat, but their military records do not reflect it. This is the story of just ONE such veteran. This is a story of a soldier who possessed the physical abilities of an exceptional athlete, coupled with the gift of a photographic memory.

In 1995, Frank experienced a major flashback in which he relived the traumatic events of a military mission in Germany. The impact of this flashback crippled his ability to sustain a steady job, and consequently, elevated his desire to write this book. The flashback also affected his ability to remember events in their entirety. Over the last three years, through both mine and his son Ray's inquiries, Frank has begun to piece together recollections with detailed clarity.

My husband and Frank both participated in the same PTSD group in 1996, and their bond is one of brothers.

Frank has been denied Veterans Administration (VA) disability benefits several times; he and his wife survive on a meager income.

In assisting Frank with writing his story, I have learned without a doubt, that the men and women who serve in our military make the ultimate sacrifice, they give up what we refer to as the luxury of a "normal" life.

Etta Cavalier, M.A., GCDF
June 17, 2011

INTRODUCTION

"Seven Missions and a Death Wish"

My name is Frank E. Wiggins and I was born in Cuba, New Mexico, on October 10th 1939. I began my enlistment in the New Army Green on February 3rd, 1958, out of Fort Ord, California. At the time, I stood at 5'6," weighed 108 pounds, was still single, had completed only three years of high school, and lived on Seymour Street in San Jose, California.

I was only seventeen when I went to enlist at the recruitment center in Oakland, California. But because I was still underage, they put me on what is known as a 'Delay Entry' program until I turned eighteen. I turned eighteen on October 10th 1957, but it was not until months later, that Uncle Sam came to claim their property.

By December of 1958, I had completed boot camp, and then advanced training at Fort Sill Oklahoma. I was selected for additional intensive training during the time I was at Fort Devens, Massachusetts, and in Ansbach, Germany. When I arrived in Ansbach, I was stationed at Darby Concern Barracks, and assigned to Battery A, 1st Howitzers Battalion, 75th Artillery, 7th Army.

By mid October of 1959, I had completed seven missions. Among other things, it mainly involved clearing mine fields in the 'Buffer Zone.' I was only eighteen years old. I was given orders which I completed for the U.S. Army to the best of my ability. After the seventh mission, I refused to participate in anymore operations. To this day, I am still reliving the trauma of that seventh mission. I have nightmares, flashbacks, and triggers that only a combat veteran would understand.

I was diagnosed with chronic PTSD (Post Traumatic Stress Disorder), on June 30, 1995, and participated in a PTSD program at the Veterans Hospital in Albuquerque, New Mexico. From the years 1960 to 1995, I knew something was wrong, however, I didn't know it as an illness, a wound in the heart and mind that is not visible.

Although I'm getting help for combat related PTSD, the nightmares still continue. I realized after the first mission I was involved in covert operations, but what I didn't know, is what the covert operation entailed or the intent of what each mission would or would not accomplish. After leaving the military, I led a nomadic and reckless life. I had a "Death Wish" and I had "No Fear." I did not plan for things to happen the way they did. It just happened.

Throughout the years, various individuals have encouraged me to write my story. I tried unsuccessfully on several occasions, but it was not until my son Ray's persistent encouragement and support, that this book began to take life.

Ray's inquiring voice weaves in and out of my story as he helps me remember events I wanted to forget and shut away forever. My wife and children lived this perilous life with me, and have stood by me all these years. They too, have been profoundly affected by my PTSD. I can never express the fullness of my love and gratitude to them for standing by me.

I am also writing this book, not just to tell my story, but to help other veterans tell their story. Whether it is as far back as the Cold War, Vietnam, Desert Storm, Iraq, Afghanistan, or as the result of participating in secret or covert operations, their story needs to be heard. I've learned that telling our story is important for our healing.

Frank E. Wiggins

Seven Steps To Hell and Back

1

I BELONGED TO UNCLE SAM

"No Turning Back"

I was up early today. I couldn't believe I had already eaten breakfast. Usually I didn't get up until nine-thirty or ten o'clock because of new medication I had recently started taking. About three weeks ago, the VA (Veterans Administration Hospital) started me on an experimental drug for high blood pressure. Interestingly enough, they had discovered several side effects; one of them was it helped with nightmares, and that was good.

The other side effect was not so good; if I didn't get at least ten to twelve hours of sleep I would wake up nauseous and dizzy. But today I had pushed myself to get up early. It was a warm fall morning and from inside my mobile home, I could hear the happy chatter of birds on the tree outside my kitchen window.

All of a sudden, the rambling of my thoughts was interrupted when I heard the front door swing open; it was my son Ray greeting me with a big smile.

"Good morning, Dad."

"Hey, Ray," I said.

"Did you already eat breakfast?' Ray asked.

"Just finished," I answered.

Ray owned a janitorial and maid service business and was returning to the house from his first job of the morning, he seemed excited about something.

Ray poured himself a cup of coffee then sat down at the

kitchen table.

"Dad, I just came from this man's house, one of my clients. You're not going to believe this, but he's a movie producer. We've talked several times while waiting for my crew to finish cleaning his house, and the last time we talked, I mentioned to him some of the things you've done in your life.

"I don't know how we got on the subject today, but we started talking about the projects in Santa Fe and I mentioned to him some of the things you did in parks in Los Angeles when you first got out of the army. I told him how you cleaned up the parks of all those gangs.

"He's very interested in you, Dad, especially after I told him more of the stuff you did when we lived in the housing projects years ago here in Santa Fe. He was asking me lots of questions and I told him about how HUD had hired you as a maintenance man, and soon afterwards, when they noticed you weren't afraid of the gangs, they asked you to take care of security for the entire housing projects. I described to him how the gangs in the housing projects controlled the neighborhoods and how you were able to stop the violence and drug dealing.

"He wants to meet you, Dad, especially after I told him how you used to fight ten to twenty guys at one time, single handed! And win!

"'How was he able to do that? What kind of training did your father have? What made him so fearless?' The producer asked me all kinds of questions. I told him you were Special Forces in the Seventh Army and that you served in Germany disarming landmines. Dad, he's really interested in your life story and wants to know if you could write a book about all that stuff, he thinks it would make a good movie.

2

"Here…" Ray handed me a piece of paper, "This is his name… he wants you to call him right away."

I sat back in my chair and glanced at the paper. Ray knew I had tried to write my story a few times before, but things always got in the way. My children had helped me write a few stories. One time I even hired a writer but I think she freaked out with some of the things I told her and she took it upon herself to change the stories into fairytales. I didn't like that so I fired her.

I began to feel nauseous just thinking of writing about my missions in Germany. Thinking about that stuff gave me anxiety.

I said to Ray, "Yeah, back in those days I had a death wish … I didn't fear anything or anybody. I wanted to die, but in my mind, whoever challenged me or wanted to hurt or kill me, had to earn it."

"Dad, I know in the past you haven't wanted to talk that much about the things you did in the Army," Ray said excitedly, "but this man is very interested in your life story. He said you're a very unique man and he's very interested in hearing about the training you had in the military because it must have prepared you to do what you did with the gangs."

Ray waited quietly; he was almost at the edge of his chair waiting for my response. Finally he asked, "Is it Okay if I start to record our conversations?" I nodded my head in approval.

I realized that just until a few years ago I had never skipped my daily workouts. Since the military, I had always been fit and for thirty-five years, I kept up my own training. I did push-ups, sit-ups; duck walks, calisthenics, kicking, and shadow boxing. I still can't believe I did this for two hours every night for thirty-five years. In my mind I had to be combat ready, twenty-four seven. It was impossible for me to let my guard down. I had only served one year, eleven months and thirteen days, but the training I endured and the things I did while on missions in the military, changed my life forever.

"Hello!" I heard Ray's voice reeling me back from my trance, "Dad, are you okay?"

I looked at him and felt blessed. All my six kids had been profoundly affected by the dangerous lifestyle I had led. I owed it to them to write this book and try to make some money. I owed it to veterans just like me. If other veterans knew my story, maybe it would help them tell their story. I especially owed it to my wife.

"Yes, I think it's time." I said to Ray.

"Alright!" he quickly responded, "Let's go buy a good digital recorder."

A week later, we sat at the kitchen table ready to get started.

"Where were you living when you went into the Army?" Ray asked.

"Well, let's see…It was 1957 when I enlisted, but that wasn't exactly when I went in. My parents had just moved to Wilmington, California from San Jose. At the time, I was sixteen and my Dad and I were not in good terms. My dad was a hard man. His friends and family called him 'Iron Man'. They said he was a mean fighter -- one punch and you were out!

"Many years later, when I used to work for the housing projects in Santa Fe, I had a partner named Lucky and he used to call me, 'One Punch Kill'! My brothers were the same, really strong. It seems like I got some of those 'fists of iron' from my Dad.

"One time, I actually got to see my Dad fight in a bar. My mom had sent me to look for him, and when I got to the bar, I looked through the bar window. I saw him and one of his friends beating up a dozen or so men."

"Why do you think your dad was that way?" Ray asked.

"From what I know, my father and his brother grew up without a father. My dad met his father only once when he was about twelve years old. It's kind of a complicated story. My father was raised by his mother and her family, but his mother died when he was very young. After her death my dad lived a rough life and I think that's what shaped his aggressive character."

"How was it growing up with your dad?" Ray asked.

"It was not easy, he believed that once his children turned seventeen, it was time for them to be on their own, and I wasn't spared."

"What happened?" Ray asked.

"We were still living in San Jose, California when I quit high school, just three months before I was supposed to graduate. I was barely sixteen years old."

"Why did you quit school?"

"I was bored."

Ray looked puzzled and asked, "Did you say you were sixteen when you were a senior?"

"Yes, I had earned enough credits. Even though I missed a lot of school, I was still able to pass all my tests. I think my counselor knew I was bored and so they let me get ahead by taking extra courses, and that's how I was able to become a senior at sixteen. I could read a book, remember everything, and pass the test with one-hundred percent! One teacher even accused me of cheating because I got all the answers right."

"Why did you quit if everything was so easy for you?" Ray asked.

"I was still bored. I met with the principal and told him I wanted to drop out and he said I couldn't, so I withdrew and enrolled at San Jose High School. They didn't let me quit either. I had no idea that all I had to do was to stop attending school.

"Not too long after I quit school, my family moved to Wilmington, a suburb of Los Angeles. We had only lived there a few months when my father told me to pack my clothes and leave. He didn't have to tell me twice. I didn't have a car so I hitch- hiked all the way from L.A. back to San Jose. I was seventeen.

"At first I lived with my sister, Mildred and brother-in-law, Joe. I had grown up in San Jose and when I arrived, I met up with two of my buddies from elementary school, George and Simon. We had lots of fun for a while but without a job or a car, I didn't have much going for me and neither did George or Simon. It was George and Simon's great idea to go enlist in the Army and so we all went to the induction center in Oakland. We heard this was the induction center where we could enlist in the New Army Green.

"By now I was seventeen, but I still needed my mother's signature to enlist. Even so, the army let me swear in, they said I could get my mother's signature later. I didn't know they had signed me up in a delay entry program.

"The army recruiter told me, 'If you can't get your mother's signature don't worry, come back the minute you turn eighteen. We already have your signature, you're already sworn in.'

"I was happy until I found out that Simon and George had chickened out! It was their idea to enlist and I was the only one who went through with it."

"Were you looking forward to going in the Army?" Ray asked.

"No way," I said without hesitation. "Just before I turned eighteen things were starting to pick up for me. I had moved three or four times since returning to San Jose and now lived with my sister, Annabelle and her husband Bob.

"When I finally turned eighteen I didn't want to go to the Army anymore. I had a car, a good construction job, and money in my pocket. My brother-in-law had a friend, a construction supervisor named Kenny, and he hired me."

"What kind of work did you do for him?" Ray asked.

"Carpentry, I had earned a carpentry certificate before dropping out of high school."

I could see the surprise on Ray's face, "How did you do that?"

"I earned it when I attended Lincoln High School. I had signed up for a carpentry program at San Jose City College that was part of the high school's vocational program. I could learn real fast and was done before anyone else in my class. I finished all the projects way ahead of time and so the instructor gave me the exam three months early, and I passed. That was before I dropped out."

"Did Kenny know you had a carpentry certificate?"

"I told him when he hired me, but he didn't believe me.

"After I was working there a short time, Kenny realized I could do a lot of things and pretty soon he promoted me to foreman. At first, the older men didn't like taking orders from such a young punk because they thought I didn't know the business. I could understand why they felt that way. I had to show them I knew the business. It didn't take me long to get their respect."

"So what did you do when you turned eighteen?"

"Well, the Army kept sending me letters but I didn't pay any attention to them. I just put them aside and the pile kept getting

7

bigger and bigger. I never once opened or read a single letter. Then one day in February, they came for me."

"Who came for you?" Ray asked

"The Military Police (MP) I can still remember that day. It changed my life forever.

"I was working on the roof of a house at a construction site. As I lifted my head, I saw a military jeep parked next to the construction site office with the letters 'MP' written on the front and back. At first, I couldn't figure out why they were there. Kenny, my boss, came out of the office and was followed by these two guys in military uniform. Kenny jumped into the back of their jeep and they drove towards my job site. I leaned back down and kept working, but at the same time, kept an eye in the direction the jeep was coming from.

"When they arrived at my building, Kenny motioned for me to come down. I got off the roof and walked over to them. The MP's got out of their jeep and walked up to me.

"One of them approached and asked, 'Are you Frank Wiggins?'

"And I said, 'Yeah.'

"'Frank E. Wiggins?' He asked again.

"'Yeah' I answered again.

"'We got a warrant to pick you up. You are A. W. O. L.'

"Kenny looked at me; he had a big smile on his face. As a veteran of the Navy he knew what the MP's had come for. He didn't even say a word as he watched the MP's handcuff me.

"Before I knew it, they had strapped a big thick leather belt around my waist and buckled it. Attached to the right and left side of this belt were two short chains which, before I knew it, they clipped to my handcuffs. Next came the ankle bracelets! "Click,

Click!" They were on. The MP's pulled out a three foot chain and connected the ankle bracelets to a hook in front of the leather belt.

"I was completely shackled before I had time to realize what was really happening to me. Sweat started to drip down my forehead. I tried to wipe it off but my hands didn't reach. A chain also connected my handcuffs to the hook on the front of the leather belt!

"I looked up in confusion and asked, 'Is this legal?' One of the MP's answered,

"'You belong to the United States Army, son. You are A.W.O.L. (Absent With-Out Leave). We should shoot you, but you're not really violent.'

"They walked me over to the back of the jeep, strapped me tight to the seat, and that's the last time I saw that job. I didn't see Kenny again until ten years later.

"The cold wind hit my face as we headed down the highway. We had already been driving about two hours when the sun disappeared below the horizon.

"It was getting real cold and I shouted out, 'When are we gonna get there? Where are we going?'

"One of the MP's shouted back, 'We're going to Fort Ord!' And that's the last time they spoke to me until we got there."

"Where's Fort Ord?" Ray asked.

"By Monterrey, near the coast," I answered.

"What happened next?"

"When the jeep drove into the base, I saw buses loaded with all kinds of guys. They must have been new recruits. The MP's kept driving on.

"'Where are you taking me?' I asked them, I wanted to know why we didn't stop."

"'We have to take you to the battalion commander's headquarters.'

"I wasn't sure what that meant but it sounded important. The jeep came to a quick stop and I thought, 'Looks like we arrived at headquarters.' Hundreds of soldiers were milling around in front of the building. Most of the guys weren't in uniform.

"The MP's jumped out and unstrapped me from the back of the jeep and walked me over to a guy I thought was an officer. Later I learned he was a Sergeant. I was still handcuffed and shackled. The officer had me escorted to a bus with other recruits; the bus was headed to the other side of the base. As I boarded I barely had enough chain on the ankle shackles to climb the steps. I sat down and looked out the window. I couldn't believe the endless flow of buses I saw arriving on the base.

"We were almost at the other side of the base when the bus began to swerve. There was loud banging coming from outside the bus. A bunch of soldiers, they must have been officers, surrounded us and were hitting the bus, banging the sides with their fists and hands. The driver was in on the whole commotion. He jerked the steering wheel causing the bus to swerve abruptly left and right. Bang! Bang! The noise echoed loudly inside the bus.

"'Wow!' I thought, 'What the heck is going on?' The bus came to a complete stop.

"One of the officers yelled, "Everyone! Get out!" "Everyone...! Right Now! Get in front of the bus!"

"I shuffled slowly behind everyone else. They kept screaming at us from every direction as we all attempted to line up in a hurry. This one really tall sergeant, who was yelling the most, walked up in front of me. I looked up and all I could see was his shiny belt buckle. I couldn't straighten up my body because the chain attached to my ankle bracelet was so tight.

"He took one step closer to me and yelled, 'Are you a troublemaker or what?'

"'No' I answered.

"'I said….! Are you a troublemaker?'

"'No, I'm not a troublemaker.' I repeated.

"He looked at me real pissed off, and said, 'I Am **A** Sergeant! When you talk to me, call me Sergeant!'

"'Yes sir, I will!'

"A sharp frown formed on his face and his eyes widen as he repeated. 'I said! I --AM --A --SERGEANT!'

"'Yes Sergeant!' I finally got it right.

"The sergeant had someone come over and take off my chains and handcuffs. I straightened up and began stretching and rubbing my wrists, when I noticed a bunch of the new recruits staring strangely at me. They thought I was someone dangerous. The whole commotion with me and the Sergeant (and the fact that I was handcuffed and shackled) created some fear in them of me. I can't say that perception was all bad. From the start, their fear earned me some respect."

Ray sat comfortably in his chair, the voice recorder propped on the table. "Wow Dad, that wasn't your usual enlistment, was it?"

"No it wasn't, son."

"Dad, after the MP's took you from your work site, you said, you didn't see Kenny until about ten years later; where did you see him the next time?"

"Let's see … I saw him in 1969, way after I had come home from the Army. One day, out of the blue, he came to my

11

shop. My brother-in-law, Bob, told him I was starting up my own chrome plating shop and that I needed some work done. Kenny came to the shop and wired the whole place for me. He put in all the electrical wiring, outlets and other stuff and never charged me a penny. He was a good friend, and I was lucky to have known a guy like him."

Ray looked surprised, "You mean he came just to do that stuff for you?"

"He sure did, he installed everything that needed to be done in order for the plating shop to pass inspection. He was a damn good friend!"

Ray and I talked for a while and then he had to leave. In the next two weeks I didn't see much of him because his business was starting to pick up and that was a good thing. More than ever I wanted to write this book, and lately, I was beginning to remember lots of things. I wanted to record these memories while they were still fresh on my mind. I needed to learn how to use a computer and try to write down some stories myself.

Willie, my other son, also lived with me and Lenora in our mobile home. Willie had mentioned some time ago about a computer software program which recorded voice and converted it to text. If so, that would be great! I knew very little about computers and accepted that it was going to take a lot of focus on my part, especially learning a software program. I was determined! Once I put my mind to something, I could do it!

During the next week, Willie and I shopped around and we finally found the right one. It was complicated; the program had to recognize my speech enunciation, but once it did, I actually was able to talk into the microphone and record. Sometimes in the middle of the day, when no one else was around, I'd remember something worth recording. I went to the computer and began to talk about the recollection. Many times afterwards, especially when I tried real hard to remember details, I would get exhausted and had to take a nap. Pretty soon I had a good collection. Willie had showed me how to save each story so I could email it to my good friend Etta, who was writing my book!

Three weeks later, Ray and I sat down at the kitchen table to continue taping where we had left off.

"Dad," Ray asked, "how long were you at Fort Ord?"

"Oh, it seemed like I was there a long time, but actually, it was only eight weeks. It was easy for me, but for some guys it wasn't."

"Why's that?"

"Well," I continued, "during the first two weeks of boot camp I heard sobbing and crying at night, it was a guy that bunked a couple of racks over from me. He was really home sick, which wasn't good. He was teased and harassed constantly by a group of guys. One night, they decided to give him a blanket party."

"A blanket party…. what's that?"

"That's when the guys fill socks with bars of soap," I said grinning. "They wait until the lights are turned off then sneak over to a guys bunk and surround it. Then they grab his blanket from all sides and cover him with it real tight. Each man takes a turn hitting the guy with the heavy socks filled with bar soap. The poor kid was all bruised up the next morning. I finally got real tired of their bullying so one night, as I heard them approaching the kid's bunk; I quietly jumped off my rack and snuck up on them. I beat them all up. I walked over to the young soldier and whispered, 'Listen kid….. If you're gonna cry, do it quietly.' He really appreciated that I stuck up for him."

"Where did you learn how to fight, Dad?"

"I learned from my brother, Ben."

"Was your brother Ben a tough guy?"

"He sure was." I answered with a grin. "He was a real good boxer. Even before I went to boot camp, I already knew how to fight pretty good thanks to Ben."

"Was Ben older than you?"

"Yeah, Ben was about 13 years older. When I was a little boy, I'd say about five, he found me crying at the bus stop. It was my first day of school.

"He walked up to me and asked, 'Why are you crying?'

"I could barely answer him, 'The boys were making fun of me and beat me up because my name is Francis.'

"I looked up at my brother and pleaded, 'Ben, teach me how to fight…..you're a boxer, teach me how to fight!'

"I asked Ben over and over again until finally he said, 'Okay! Okay! Tonight I'll take you with me; we're going to a boxing match.'

"Sure enough, that evening he took me with him and, to my surprise, Ben put me in the ring that very night, and with a much bigger kid. I was so scared; I thought I was going to get really beat up. Ben knew I was scared. I looked at him and my eyes were as wide as could be. As Ben was putting my boxing gloves on, he leaned down and whispered in my ear very seriously, 'You better not cry! If you do, I'm gonna beat you up myself! I'll beat the crap out of you on our way home, understand?' I shook my head in acknowledgement.

"He showed me a few moves then said, 'When you're in the ring, just swing like a windmill. The minute the other kid thinks you're gonna box, he'll get up close to you, and that's when you windmill him! Understand? You got plenty of time to learn.'

"During the first round we just touched gloves here and there. Then in the second round, the kid came up close to me, like he was ready to box. I heard Ben's voice in my head say, 'Windmill him!' and I did. My arms were all over the place and before I knew it, I couldn't see the kid. I looked down and he was on the mat. And so began my fighting days." Ray and I were laughing, imaging how I must have looked standing there swinging my arms all over the place.

"Was boot camp hard?"

I grinned at Ray as he asked me that question. "No, it was fun and the time went by fast. Aside from all the training, everyone in boot camp gets KP duty or guard duty each week."

"What's KP stand for?"

"It's short for, 'kitchen police' or working in the chow hall.

"After boot camp I was supposed to go to Fort Macarthur but they changed my orders. At the last minute, I was shipped to Fort Sill, Oklahoma."

"What happened? Why were your orders changed?"

"I'm not sure why. A few weeks before the end of boot camp, most of us knew where we were being stationed. My orders read Fort MacArthur. I was excited because Fort MacArthur was in San Pedro and that was near Harbor City, where my parents lived.

"I hadn't used any days off during boot camp so I had fifteen days of furlough coming, five from boot camp, and ten given after boot camp, before reporting to our duty station. I decided to take five days and check out Fort MacArthur. I wanted to get a jump and see if I could get a locker ahead of time."

"Why?" Ray asked.

"Because I wanted to leave some of my gear in a locker. I was always thinking ahead.

"I arranged for a ride on a military jeep from Fort Ord to Moffett Field Air Force Base. Moffett Field was just north of San Jose. At Moffett Field I would be able to catch a 'Hop' to the nearest Naval Air Force Base near Fort MacArthur."

"A Hop… What's that?"

"All Air Force Bases have flights a soldier can catch to another Base, they're real cheap. You just have to put in for it, show up, and see if there's room for you on the flight.

"When I got to Fort MacArthur, the Command couldn't find my orders. They called Fort Ord and found out my duty station was changed. I was disappointed."

"Why?"

"I was hoping to go to Fort MacArthur because it was closer to my home."

"What happened after you found out that wasn't your duty station?"

"I was still on furlough so I asked a military jeep to give me a ride home to Harbor City. They dropped me off a block from my parent's house.

"During the five days I was home, I visited with my friends and family and had a good time. I visited your mother; we knew each other before I went into the Army." I started grinning.

"What's so funny?" Ray asked.

"When I saw your mom, she gave me a pair of gold leaf earrings and pinned them on the shoulders of my uniform. She said they were for good luck so I left them on my uniform and left to my mother's house. It just so happened that my brother Ben was visiting from San Jose and was at my parent's house too.

"At the end of my furlough, he gave me a ride back to Fort Ord. Your uncle Ben left me off at the entry gates of the base. As I walked on base, several soldiers saluted me. I was puzzled, 'Why did he salute me?' I thought.

"I continued to walk in and another soldier saluted me. 'What's going on?' I thought. I stopped, looked up and down at my uniform. That's when I discovered that on my shoulders were the gold leaf earrings your mom had pinned on me, they looked like a Lieutenant Colonel's insignia. I grinned mischievously and decided to keep them on just to have a little more fun. As I walked into the barracks a group of my buddies were about to call everyone to attention when they realized it was only me.

"'You're crazy, Wiggins! You could get a court martial for impersonating an officer.' I just laughed and took the earrings off."

"Sounds like you made it fun, Dad."

"I tried!"

"During the whole time of boot camp I only worked two KP's. I did one at the beginning of the eight weeks and the other one on the last day of boot camp." I smiled at Ray and he knew there was more to the story. "There was another soldier named Bill Wiggin, not Wiggins with an 's' like me. One week before we completed boot camp, both of us got a weekend pass and I invited him to San Jose with me.

"On the way, we were talking and he said, "Boy, they've been giving me guard and KP duty a lot! I thought we were supposed to pull guard and KP only once a week!"

"I turned my head and stared at him, without saying a word, I thought, "That poor guy!" I could hardly keep from laughing as he kept talking. The reason I hadn't been pulling KP and guard duty the whole time during boot camp, was because Bill had been taking my orders first. Bill was always in line before me. Since Wiggin came before Wiggins, he took his orders, and the next time around, took mine too by mistake. I was always right behind him and nothing was ever there for me. I told myself, 'Oh well, I'm not going to ruin a good thing by asking why.'"

"That's why he never got a break!" Ray said laughing.

"Yeah," we were both laughing hard. "Anyway, after we came back from our weekend pass I wanted to fix it. I thought, 'This is a nice guy, I sure don't want that to happen to him again.'"

"So how did you fix it?" Ray asked.

"I told them." I answered.

"Who did you tell?"

"I had to tell the drill instructor, he was the one who assigned everyone their duty. I let him know I had only pulled one KP." I started laughing and continued, "As a matter of fact, I also told him that I hadn't pulled any guard duty either.

"What did he say when you told him?" Ray asked.

"'Are you sure?' he said. 'Maybe they made a mistake.'

"The Sergeant then went to the office to check and their records showed I had been doing both. Well, with only one week left of boot camp, I made sure to get up early that Monday and beat Bill to the lineup for our orders. When I looked at them, it was my turn to pull guard duty. I didn't know what to expect, it was my first time.

"I rushed over trying to get into formation quickly before the officers began their inspection. Two officers walked around inspecting every soldier as we stood at attention. I was paying close attention.

"They randomly selected soldiers for inspection. I noticed that when the Sergeant and Lieutenant stood in front of a soldier, the soldier would salute the Officer with his rifle, 'Present Arms!' The two then proceeded to walk behind the ranks. They inspected each soldier's haircut, uniform and gear. I didn't know they were going to inspect our bayonets.

"It was my luck that the young Lieutenant stopped behind me first. He reached for my bayonet. I was supposed to unclip the sheath securing the bayonet so the Lieutenant could remove it easily to inspect.

"Like I said," I grinned at Ray, "I didn't know the routine since I hadn't pulled any guard duty. He reached for my bayonet, and I thought I was being attacked. Before I could stop my reflexes, I had flung the rifle over my head and in a split second bashed the young Lieutenant in the mouth with the butt of my rifle! I tried to restrain the blow when I realized what I was doing, but it was too late. The Sergeant tried to break the Lieutenant's fall, but he still hit the ground."

Ray looked at me almost at the edge of his chair, "Wow Dad, did you get in trouble for that?"

I laughed then continued with the story. "Right away I could hear the entire squad. Their voices went… 'Ahhh…Oh Shit!' The Lieutenant got up. He looked at me surprised. You could see he was shaken up. But to my surprise, he didn't do anything."

Ray's eyes widened, "Wow, what happened next? Did you get in trouble?"

"No, but I still had to pull guard duty that day. You're supposed to pull guard two hours on, and two hours off. Someone takes your place while you rest on your two hours off. Two hours later, it starts all over again until five o'clock in the morning.

"I had just finished my first shift when that same Lieutenant I hit approached me. He stopped right in front of me, looked me square in the eye and rubbed his jaw. His jaw was still red from the butt of my rifle.

"'You did well soldier. You reacted in a manner that showed you learned all that we have been training you for. You're relieved for the night.'

"Then he handed me a paper. I stood there surprised as hell with the realization I didn't have to pull anymore guard duty that night. And to top it off, he gave me a three day pass."

Ray couldn't believe it either. "How lucky can that be?"

"I know," I smiled. "I had just come back from a five day furlough. And now, I had three more days off! I was happy! It was the last week of boot camp and now I didn't have to report back until Thursday night.

"On Friday, my last day, I reported for KP duty. The cook was really pissed off."

"Why?"

"Because he found out from the Staff Sergeant that I had only pulled one KP the whole time I was in boot camp. It was the last day and he was mad, he wanted to make it rough for me the entire day. By five o'clock in the morning, I was frying eggs - lots of eggs! For lunch, I was frying chicken. I never saw so many damn chickens in my life. I served chicken until 2 pm and then started getting ready for dinner.

"The cook was riding me. He told me to peel potatoes for dinner. He told me to put them in this big drum that was a potato peeler, but didn't show me how to use it.

"'Put the potatoes in it, and they'll be ready!'

"And so I did. I emptied a fifty pound bag of potatoes into the potato peeler. He also didn't tell me exactly how long to leave the potatoes in the drum. I had no idea how long it would take for the machine to peel all those potatoes. I clamped the drum lid tight, flipped the switch on, and went for a quick walk around the big kitchen. I was fascinated by all the big pots, pans and everything else. Thirty minutes later, I returned to check on the potatoes. I opened the drum and bah! No more potatoes! Someone was playing a joke on me. They must have taken the potatoes and hid them. I looked all around but didn't see anyone. The heck with it! I put another fifty pound bag of potatoes into the drum. This time I stayed right there checking every few minutes. After five minutes, I opened the drum. To my surprise, all the potatoes were peeled.

"The cook continued to ride me all afternoon. He didn't let up one bit. But I got back at him."

"What did you do, Dad?"

I smiled mischievously at Ray.

"Well, at the end of each day, two officers come around to do inventory. A First Lieutenant and a Warrant Officer check the supplies used that day. It's their job to make sure everything is accounted for. There has to be enough supplies ready for the next day. After taking inventory, they noticed a fifty pound sack of potatoes was missing. They searched all over the place but couldn't find it.

"'We're missing a fifty pound sack of potatoes, where is it?' they asked the cook. The cook turned to me,

"'Wiggins! Where is it?'

"'I have no idea sir!' I innocently shrugged my shoulders as if I didn't know. I was going to say something but decided not to. That cook had made the day so miserable for me that I thought this was fair game. I really did think someone had played a joke on me and taken the potatoes out of the drum. Later I realized the potatoes had actually disintegrated!

"The cook got in big trouble for those potatoes. He was still mad at me, and to get even, didn't release me from KP duty until real late that night. I ran to my barracks to grab my duffle bag and pack all my gear. I was hoping my ride hadn't left and rushed over to Company Headquarters to pick up orders for my next duty station.

"By the time I got there, the place was already secured for the day. Everyone else had picked up their orders and left. I ran over to Battalion Headquarters, my orders would be there. I rushed like a mad man. They handed me my orders, and that's when I noticed Fort Macarthur had been lined out with a thick black marker. Fort Sill, Oklahoma was now my duty station. I didn't have time to dwell on my disappointment. I had to run and catch my ride home. I barely made it."

"So who gave you a ride home, Dad?"

"The same kid who cried at night at the beginning of boot camp. His father came from LA to pick us up.

"We reached LA and the father insisted I have dinner with them, and so I did. They lived in a huge beautiful home. Obviously, they had lots of money. After dinner, the kid's father handed me $400 in cash."

"That was a lot of money in those days. Why did he give you that much money?"

"I think it was because I stuck up for his son during boot camp. He also handed me a paper. Written on it was his name, address and telephone number.

"'Here,' he said. 'In case you ever need anything. Thank you for being there for my son.'"

"Dad, I know you're a real prankster. I'm sure you enjoyed getting back at the KP cook. Did you play jokes on anyone else?"

"Oh yeah, everyone did at one time or another. After boot camp I went back to playing jokes on anyone I could."

Figure 1 - Fort Ord, California, Frank E. Wiggins, 1958
(Boot Camp Photo)

2

SPECIALIZED TRAINING

"O.D. Green"

"My furlough had come to an end. I had three days left and told my family I had to leave immediately. I had planned to hitch hike all the way to my next duty station in Fort Sill, Oklahoma. It would take me at least three days to get there. Willie, my brother, didn't want me to hitch hike. He wanted me to stay a few more days and so he bought me an airplane ticket. I stayed two more days then caught a flight out of San Francisco to Denver. From there I boarded a small engine plane that took me to Oklahoma.

"The base at Fort Sill, Oklahoma specialized in field artillery training and it was there that I first learned how to operate 105 millimeter Howitzer's."

"How long was your training?" Ray asked.

"You mean on the Howitzers?"

"Yeah,"

"All the time I was there. Even when I got to Germany, the training never really stopped."

I was tired. It had been a long afternoon. I sat back in my chair, took a deep long breath, and stared toward the kitchen window. Ray knew I was reliving another moment as he noticed the far off look in my eyes. I forced myself to continue.

"I trained for one year, maybe one year and four or five months. From the time I started advanced training, it was one thing right after another. It seemed that I trained every minute up until I started the missions.

"As soon as I arrived at Fort Sill, Oklahoma, I was given my orders. I was assigned to these barracks that were far off to one side of the main base. It was a huge base, and the barracks were located on the perimeter, right next to a freeway. I found my barracks and went inside. Finally, I saw where my bunk was and went to put my stuff away. I didn't know these barracks housed only black soldiers. I'm not sure why, but for some reason, I was the only white looking man assigned there. And let me tell you, it wasn't easy bunking there at first!"

"Why?" Ray's curiosity peeked. I had told him many stories over the years, but I don't think I ever told him about this one.

"They were all black soldiers. And they were very prejudiced against me. In those days, there was a lot of prejudice toward blacks. The white man was very cruel to them, and I definitely looked like a white man. I didn't really blame them for thinking I was white, I just happen to look like one. I took after my father's German and my mother's Spanish side of the family. I was light skinned, brown hair and light brown eyes."

"Was your mother light skinned too?"

"Yeah, she had blondish brown hair and blue eyes. Her mother was Hispanic, from New Mexico and her father was from Spain. I'll have to tell you the story later about the time I went to find that side of my family when I was stationed in Germany.

"Anyway, getting back to this one, my mother was born in New Mexico, she spoke fluent Spanish and English and a few other languages. I too spoke fluent Spanish. But I spoke English without an accent, and maybe that's why they thought I was white.

Anyways, none of us had a choice. We were all soldiers. We were there in the same boat and had to get along.

"The first day at dinner none of the black soldiers sat at my table. I had it all to myself, and that was fine with me. After dinner, everyone walked out of the chow hall and stood around outside the barracks.

"Just then, the national anthem came over the loud speakers. Everyone quickly stood at attention and saluted the flag as it was being lowered. As I was standing there, I got this strange feeling I was under a microscope. Slowly, I managed to move my eyes from side to side. First to the left, and then to the right! Sure enough, every single black soldier had their eyes fixed on me. No one said a single word. I guess you could say, there was definitely an element of mistrust focused on me.

"It was time to turn in and I headed back to the barracks. Upon opening the barrack door, I couldn't believe what I saw. The scene was like something you would only see in a Hollywood movie. It was hilarious! The black soldiers had moved all their bunks to the left side of the squad bay. Mine was the only bed that remained on the other side. I smiled, 'Okay, more room for me!'"

Ray and I both had a big laugh.

"What happened next?"

"Everything went fine for a few days. Then one afternoon, a young black soldier swaggered confidently over toward my side. I was sitting on my bunk polishing my boots but also aware that he was slowly approaching. I kept polishing my boots. He got closer. I could tell he was feeling pretty brave and wanted to fight. He stopped right in front of me and just as I stood up he took a swing. It was a right cross and I blocked it immediately! Before he knew what happened, I countered with a swift right upper cut square on his chin. In an instant, he was knocked out cold. The guy didn't even know what hit him. He lay sprawled out on the floor with his head under my bunk. I knew some of his buddies were following right behind him, but I was ready for them too.

"I slowly turned around anticipating some more trouble. They stood there wide eyed, obviously surprised at seeing their friend knocked out cold. I said calmly, 'I don't want to hurt anybody. We're on the same side.'

"Everyone stayed real quiet. No one said a word. 'Well, what are you waiting for? Come and help your friend!' A couple of them walked over and lifted him to his feet. After this, we kept to our own business.

"Within the next few weeks I began intense training. I learned hand-to-hand combat, artillery, and even began learning how to detonate and disarm landmines. Whatever our commander felt I needed to know, I learned it.

"In the meantime, I thought everything was resolved between me and the blacks. I was wrong. It was a Saturday morning and I had gotten up real early. I had already showered and was dressed to go out. I was just waiting to get picked up by my Sergeant. He was taking a group of us dancing."

Ray grinned, "Dancing….early in the morning?"

"Yeah, I know it sounds funny, but on Saturdays, our hand-to-hand combat instructor took us dancing. He said it was part of our training.

"I remember his saying, *'If you can dance all night, you can fight all day!'*" Ray and I had a good laugh.

"Anyway, I was lying down on my bunk, waiting for my ride when out of nowhere a big black man appeared in front of me. I slowly got up. He was tall and stood in front of me flexing his muscles. This guy was pretty big and fit, but I knew I could take him.

"With a cocky grin he tells me, 'Today you meet a man!'

"'I don't want to hurt you.' I answered.

"He raised his eyebrows, 'Oh, so you really think I'm that easy? Well come and get some!'

"Right then he threw a kick. I caught his foot between my hands, and with my right foot, countered with a high kick right to his chest. It landed just below his throat. I thrust that kick hard! I didn't want to hurt the guy but I had to stop him. He immediately fell on his back and landed flat on the floor.

"Shocked, he raised his head and sat up quickly. 'Okay I give up, don't hit me again! Let me stand up!'

"I let him get up, but kept a close eye on his every move. He walked over toward my bunk and sat down rubbing his throat. His buddies were anxiously watching us to see what would happen next.

"I turned to them and said, 'Don't fight with me! I already told you guys. We're on the same side!' Quietly, they all left.

"I had been assigned to an ammunition dump when I first arrived at Fort Sill and was on my way to work the following morning when I saw one of the black guys from my barracks headed in my direction. We both happen to train at the same ammunition dump. We wound up walking next to each other.

"'Do you mind if I walk with you?' he asked.

"I didn't hold anything against him, and so we ended up going to work together. At the end of the week, he and I had a beer at the PX, we actually began to get to know each other.

"I started the conversation first, 'I'm from California, from Los Angeles and San Jose.' Pausing a bit, I continued. 'I know you may see me as being prejudiced, but I don't see you that way. I don't see you as being different. Growing up I've always had black friends.'

"It took him a little while to finally let his guard down. 'You wouldn't believe the prejudice I've lived through all my life' he confided.

"'I really do understand!' I told him. 'Last Sunday I went to a bar in Lawton. There were signs posted on the wall that read, 'No dogs or Negroes.' I shook my head, 'that's real disturbing to me.'

"From that moment on we became friends. Eventually, the rest of the Black soldiers in the barracks accepted my friendship. Some of us even became pretty good friends. Within a few weeks, I got back to having fun and playing jokes.

"Over 2,000 soldiers were assigned to that part of the base. All of them Black, except for me and the company commander. During my stay, practically all of the Black soldiers were eventually shipped out. New soldiers arrived. Most of them were White, Puerto Rican, Chicanos, some Blacks, and a few Native Americans. In the end, there were very few Blacks left.

"Fort Sill was a huge base. At the time, there were over 30,000 soldiers stationed there. I was getting used to my routine when they informed me I had new orders. The following day I went to pick them up. I was to report to some kind of testing center and when I arrived, there was already a bunch of guys waiting.

"I couldn't help but notice that almost every soldier there was white, except for me, a couple of blacks, and a Puerto Rican. We all were given a battery of tests over several days. The first day I finished mine right away and handed it to one of the officers. He looked it over and took it to the office.

"During break, one of the test administrators called me over. 'How did you finish so quickly, Wiggins? You must have cheated.'

"'And how would I have done that?' I answered. 'Where would I have gotten the answers?' They didn't let me leave. I had to sit there until the rest finished the test. There were several who finished early after me, and they had to stay too."

"Didn't you always do well on tests, Dad?"

"Yes. Since I was young, I learned quickly. I could read an entire page in a few seconds and remember every single thing. My mother could do that too, and she showed me how to organize all the information in my head. There were about ten of us who had finished our testing very early. We reported to the test center on the second day. To my surprise, the ten of us were given a three day pass to go anywhere we wanted."

"How many soldiers got tested?" Ray asked.

"I'm not really sure because as one group finished another one started. I think there must have been close to one-thousand soldiers over several days. When the tests were over, I heard only about three hundred of us passed. I didn't realize until later that all of us, who passed, were selected for special training. We were now training for the 'New Army Green Special Forces.' From that day forward, the training accelerated. I found myself having little time for anything else.

"I learned everything about the 105 millimeter Howitzer. Once a week I trained on the 105. Two days a week land mines, and the rest of the week learning hand to hand combat techniques. In between came the shooting part. I was already real good with a rifle. I had learned how to shoot since I was around seven years old."

"How did you learn how to shoot so young?" Ray asked.

"My brothers taught me. Willie, my older brother, taught me to be a real sharp shooter. We practiced shooting at little cherry plums. First, he taught me how to shoot at them with a BB gun, and when I got good, he handed me a twenty-two. I learned fast. Willie would have my little brother Joe stand about fifty feet in front of me and hold a cherry plum between his fingers and tell me to shoot it. I got so good that I could shoot it right out from between his fingers!"

"With a twenty-two….?" Ray asked surprised. "Did you ever miss?"

"No. My brother taught me well. My little brother Joe wanted to learn too. After he got good at shooting other targets, Willie had me hold the cherry plum for him. Good thing it was only the BB gun."

"What happened?"

"Joe shot me with a BB in the back of my hand. Joe wanted to use the twenty-two. Thank goodness Willie didn't let him. I also remember Willie slapping a chunk of peanut butter on a fence post in our backyard and then putting jelly on top of it.

"'Stand about forty feet away!' He shouted at me. We waited until flies landed on the sticky sweet target. 'Shoot the fly, Frank! Don't miss. Shoot the fly!'"

"Did you get it?" Ray asked eagerly.

"I sure did."

"Did your mom know what you guys were doing?"

"Are you kidding?" I answered, "She would have had a heart attack!"

"So you were pretty good at shooting even before the Army."

"I sure was. And I could tell the drill instructors were pleased because I learned everything they were teaching us fast. I had excellent vision. *If I could see it, I could shoot it!*

"The training continued non-stop, thank goodness we had Sundays off."

"Do you think that now-a-days soldiers are better trained?" Ray asked

"No. Back then, 'Special Forces' had to learn everything. Now everyone is trained as a specialist in only one thing. I didn't realize until much later that I was Special Forces."

"What other training did they put you through?"

"One of them was learning how to maintain a gas depot."

"You mean like a gas station?" Ray asked.

"Almost, except that it was huge and stored all our fuel. I had to make sure there was always enough fuel in the pumps. We had to fill these big trucks with the gas and deliver the fuel to Howitzers which were out in the field. After I learned how to maintain a gas depot, we learned how to blow it up!"

"Why?" Ray asked.

"That was just part of the training."

"Where were the gas depots you had to blow up?"

"All the maneuvers we did were out in the Oklahoma desert."

"Dad, what's the hardest thing you learned there?"

I thought for just a minute. "How to detect and disarm land mines. That was one of the most difficult things I had to learn. We all had to develop nerves of steel. I learned that sometimes landmines have booby traps on the underside. We were taught to be extremely careful handling the device as we were putting the pin back in. It never failed. Every time as I put the pin back into the device, it would click, 'Oh my God!' I was waiting for a big bang to follow. I thought I was going to get blown up and die! People don't realize how traumatic that can be. You never get used to it even after you learn everything about land mines. To this day when I hear a, "Click," it sends me immediately into a flashback. It never fails, that same night, I have nightmares."

I started laughing and Ray looked at me with a perplexed expression. "What?" he asked.

I smiled, "Did I ever tell you what happened at Andy's mom's house about five years ago?"

"I'm not sure, what happened?" Ray answered.

"After one of our PTSD sessions at the VA, Andy invited me to his mother's house. We arrived in his Suburban truck and walked into the yard. There was dog-shit all over the ground and Andy wanted us to be careful not to step on any dog shit so he told me, **'Watch out for the landmines Franqué** (Fran-qué, Frank)**!'**

"I don't remember too much after that statement. I know we went inside to talk to his mother and then left and went back to Andy's house. When Andy had yelled out, 'Watch out for the landmines Franqué,' I had instantly lost track of time.

"It seemed like only five minutes later that I was sitting in a chair in Andy's living room. Andy noticed I was sweating like crazy just sitting there.

"He turned to his son and said, 'Maurice, bring Franqué some water please.'

"My eyes were closed as I waited for Maurice. I heard him approaching and stretched out my hand; 'Put it here, híto (Son).' It was as if I was reliving one of my missions again.

"I heard Andy say, 'Are you okay, Franqué?'

"I still had my eyes closed, 'Yeah, I'm OK, Bro. I'm just having a flashback. The landmines, you remember - at your mom's house?'

"'Oh man, I'm sorry, oh I'm so sorry!' Andy kept apologizing.

"'You didn't know. It's OK. You didn't know. I'll be alright in a few minutes. Just let me sit here awhile.'

"I sunk so deep into the flashback that I couldn't come out of it. Andy had to drive me to the VA Hospital to see my counselor, Dr. Evelyn Sandeen."

"Wow, Dad! Just that word triggered you that bad?"

"Yeah, I'm doing better now." I grinned, "And Andy knows better too! He doesn't mention landmines anymore.

"Anyway, getting back to my training….. This old guy, my instructor, he was a sergeant. I called him an old guy, because he was about forty years old and I was only eighteen. He was an expert on landmines. I had been training with him for a few weeks.

"'Look Wiggins, you're over there wasting a lot of time with that bayonet trying to find landmines. I'm gonna show you how to do it right. But first, go all the way across the field with your bayonet and try to find them all yourself.'

"I had to look for markings in the dirt to see if they were landmines and dig them out with my bayonet.

"'Go! Do it all by yourself. When you're done, I'll show you the way I do it.'

"He observed as I started. 'No! Not in a straight line. You have to zigzag your way across.' It took me all day to clear a path four feet wide through the mine field. When I finished, the old man took me over to another location that had landmines. 'Look! See this mine field? They just re-did it the other day. Look!' He pointed, 'You can see every place where they put a mine. See? The ground looks looser around those places.' He squatted down and pointed, 'Look! The wind has blown on that half of the field.' He fanned his arm across the field. 'Now see how the dirt appears? The landmines leave little indentations in the dirt and you can see clearly where they're at. Now, I want you to walk all the way across the field and not step on a single land mine.'

"'No way! I'll get blown up!'

"'No you won't!' He told me confidently. 'I'll even teach you how to run across the field and not get blown up!'

"The 'old man' had lots of patience. He went over the process again and again, but still, I couldn't see the landmines clearly. I must say, he was a good and patient instructor. The next day we were at it again. It had just snowed and he took me out to one of the mine fields.

"'I want to show you the difference in the snow.' He pointed out across the field at some landmines. 'See how the snow has melted right where the iron is? That's because the iron, the land mine, is warmer than the dirt. Tomorrow when we come back, I'm gonna show you another difference weather can make.'

"The next day I noticed the land mines appeared higher than the landscape surface. The iron was colder so the snow had built up on them. I could see all these little bumps on the field.

"'See,' he pointed across the field, 'All those are land mines! Now let's go dismantle them.'

"He taught me how to identify which ones were the 'big ones,' the 'small ones,' and the ones that could barely be seen. He then taught me how to dismantle all of them.

"'They also make little wooden ones and these are the worst! They are very hard to find, but you can do it! If you really... really.... look!'"

"Did they use a lot of wooden ones in Germany?" Ray asked.

"No, mostly what I encountered was iron. Once iron landmines are planted, someone has to check on them about every four months because they start sweating. They then start corroding and become unstable.

"Week after week the old man went over the techniques with me. That old sergeant knew everything! He even trained us in hand-to-hand combat. When it came to the landmine training, I still couldn't get what he was trying to show me. I just couldn't seem to see the land mines as clearly as he wanted me to.

"One day, I went out to a field by myself. I stood there looking at it with my eyes not really fixed on anything. All of a sudden it was as if a switch turned on in my head. 'Oh my Gosh....I can see the landmines!'

"For the first time I could see them clearly. It was as though I was looking at a kitchen table and seeing every item on it. I turned around and ran back to the base. I wanted to tell the old man that I finally got it. When I got to the base, I couldn't find him. I asked around and finally one of the officers told me he was no longer here. I had missed him by a few hours, the Sergeant had just been transferred somewhere else."

"Were you disappointed?" Ray asked.

"Yes, I was. But if he ever gets to read what I'm writing, if he is still alive, I want him to know that I learned the job really good. That's why I am still here today!"

"What did you do after that?"

"I continued training. It was constant, but I always made time for fun." Ray laughed; he knew that I loved practical jokes.

"Even as I was growing up, I played pranks on friends. I had a real good sense of humor. When I was a teenager, my friends would take me with them to parties, they actually paid me to tell jokes, and it came natural to me. Like I said, I was up to my old ways in the barracks."

"What kind of pranks did you do?"

"I short sheeted my buddies' beds and hid their pillows."

"Short sheeted?" Ray asked.

"Yeah, you get one sheet and fold it in half then make the bed. It looks like a regularly made bed with two sheets but there is only one. So when that person jumps into their bed, their legs can only go half way in because the sheet is folded in half."

Ray and I both started laughing. "It's really very funny to watch. Some guys don't even realize why they can't push their legs down. They're lying in the folded sheet and pulling on the top half. Some guys really get pissed off and start cussing and fighting with the bed sheet while the rest of the guys in the squad bay watch and laugh. It makes me laugh just thinking of it!"

"What other things did you do Dad?"

"Lots of stuff; the summers in Oklahoma were really hot and there were a lot of beetles. Our door screens were always full of beetles the size of my thumb. One time I scraped a bunch of beetles into a pillowcase, seemed like hundreds of them things. As soon as I filled that one up, I went and got another and filled that one up too."

"What did you do with them?"

"Pay back! The week before one of the guys had played a joke on me. He cut all the toes off my socks and I had to buy new ones, and that cost me money. I was waiting for the right time to get even with him and I wanted to do something really funny. I waited until Friday night when all the guys were out late getting drunk because I knew he too would be coming in drunk with them. I put the two pillowcases full of beetles under his blankets and tucked the bottom of his bed sheets tight so the beetles wouldn't get out until he went to bed. I knew that as soon as he pulled the sheet over him, the beetles would crawl out of the pillowcases.

"Sure enough… He came in drunker than a skunk! He got in his bed and pulled that sheet over his head. The beetles began coming out from under his sheet and began crawling all over his head. It was dark and the guy couldn't see a thing. He started screaming and jumped out bed, stumbling from his drunkenness. Someone turned on the lights and his face was black, it was covered with beetles. Everyone started laughing. It was the funniest thing you ever saw. The guy was stomping on the floor, stumbling and jumping up and down. He wanted someone to help him get the beetles off but no one helped. Every time he approached them, they kept backing off because they didn't want the beetles to get all over them too. Just thinking of it still makes me laugh. I think I played a joke on practically everyone in my barracks.

"Then one day it was payback! The guys got me pretty good. I still don't know how they did it without waking me. One morning I was awakened by the sound of cars and trucks. I was still lying in bed with my blankets over my face. Slowly I pulled them down and peeked out.

"'Oh God!' I said aloud. I couldn't help but laugh. "The guys had actually carried me in my bunk all the way to the end of the base. That was a good mile and half from the barracks. I could see the freeway and hear cars zooming close by. How did they do it without waking me? I hadn't been drinking the night before!

"That's a long way! I threw the blankets off and jumped off my bunk. All I had on was my underwear. I lifted my rack over my head and laughed all the way back to the barracks. I must have looked hilarious walking barefoot with only my O.D. green underwear. By the time I reached the barracks, everyone was outside in formation. They were all laughing as I walked by with the bunk on top of my head.

"Someone yelled, 'Present Arms!' and they all saluted me. I had a big smile on my face. I actually saluted them back while balancing the bunk on my head with one hand. Pay back is a bitch!" I told Ray.

"Did you get mad at them for doing that?"

"Oh no, it was fair game."

"Growing up, I pulled quite a few pranks on my friends, but I never did anything mean to someone unless they did it to me first. I was witty, funny and loved to make my friends laugh. Let me tell you about the best one of all."

"You mean there's a better one?"

"Yep, I was in my second eight weeks of training and I had a First Sergeant who wouldn't let up on me. For some reason, he had it out for me. It was morning and we all filed in for revelry, roll call and inspection. On this particular morning, the First Sergeant stopped right in front of me. I usually passed inspection but this day I accidentally left the pocket on my shirt unbuttoned.

"He put his fingers on the button and asked me 'Do you want that button?'

"'Yes sergeant!' I replied. Whack!

"He yanked it off my shirt and put it in my hand, then said, 'Sew it back on and use it properly soldier!'

"A couple of days later it happened again. I don't know how, but I left it unbuttoned again. Shit happens, son!

"Again, the First Sergeant stopped in front of me. He looked me straight in the eyes, then put his fingers in my pocket and this time he tore the entire pocket off. Only the pocket flap with the button still remained.

"'You don't need that pocket, soldier, if it's not buttoned!' He then handed me the torn pocket.

"I pretended not to care. Casually, I took the torn pocket and buttoned it to the flap still left on my shirt.

"He looked at me with a smug grin and said 'That's better soldier!'

"A couple of days passed and again we lined up for inspection. When it was my turn for inspection, the First Sergeant looked down at my boots, and proceeded to step on one of them, it got badly scuffed.

"'Your boots need shining, soldier!'

"'There was nothing wrong with my boot until you stepped on it!' I answered.

"He was taking pleasure in the situation, 'Take it to the captain and complain there!'

"'I'm not a cry baby like YOU!' I answered back. I could see his face turn red.

"Immediately one of his Lieutenants came over and looked down at my boots too. 'Your boots are scuffed, soldier!' and proceeded to write me up.

"After he wrote me up, another Lieutenant stopped in front of me. He too looked down at my boots and mockingly said, 'What happened to your boot, soldier?'

"At that point I was so mad that I wanted to get all three of them, but the one I really wanted, was the First Sergeant. I wanted to challenge him to a fight, I was well trained, and I knew I could kick his ass. It took all I had to maintain my composure. Weeks passed and the harassment continued. He knew I wanted to get him real bad.

"Several times he walked up to me and said, 'I darrrrre you!' But I waited patiently. I was planning something big. The First Sergeant had no idea what kind of revenge I had begun to put together.

"Finally, a month later the opportunity presented itself. The entire company was dispatched on a training exercise. Everyone was going to be out in the field for two weeks. Only a few soldiers, including the First Sergeant, had stayed behind. We were three days into our maneuvers when I heard that one of the trucks was going back to base for some supplies.

"No one noticed when I jumped into the back of the truck as it headed out. The truck arrived at the base and as soon as it came to a stop, I snuck back to my barracks. The guys were too busy getting supplies to notice me.

"Oh, yeah! This was the opportunity I had been waiting for. A few weeks before, I had gone to the motor pool and took some dye packets, the military used O.D. green (olive drab) to dye the seats in jeeps. I also had gone to a local drugstore and ordered some powered peroxide and hair dye. I had no idea they made powdered peroxide until the drugstore clerk told me. Perfect!

"Of course I didn't want to tell the drugstore clerk what I was up to. I asked him, 'What's the best way to dye the tail of a raccoon hat dark O.D. green?'

"He was very helpful. 'Well, I don't carry anything that is O.D. green but, he pointed to some colors, if you mix these two colors of hair dyes, you can get a very dark O.D. green.'

"'Great! That's what I want.' So he ordered the peroxide and dyes for me. When the order arrived, I mixed all the powder ingredients, put them in a container, and hid it in my foot locker."

"Weren't you afraid that someone would find them in your locker during inspection?" Ray asked.

"Oh no, I made sure they were way at the bottom of my foot locker where no one could see them.

"Anyway, as soon as I got to my barracks, I quickly got my mixture from the foot locker and snuck into the First Sergeant's barracks and then into the shower room. With a quick glance, I counted four shower heads. One by one I took them apart and filled each one with the ingredients I had mixed together. I packed the powder tight in each and every one of those shower heads and then screwed the shower heads back on."

"Why did you fill all the shower heads Dad?"

"I wanted to make sure that no matter which shower he used, the job would get done. I rushed back to the warehouse in time to sneak back into the supply truck as it was getting ready to leave. It was sure hard to hide my mischievous smile when I got back to the field, but I managed. One week of training passed before I returned with my company back to base.

"Then it happened!

"I had just walked into the barracks when one of the guys came up to me. 'Hey, Wiggins! The First Sergeant is looking for you!'

"I innocently asked 'Why?'

"'He's O.D. green! ... ALL OVER! Every single part of his body is green! The troops are calling him the green hornet! You know, like the green hornet on the radio show. He's real mad! And he's looking for you. He thinks you had something to do with it! Everyone told him you were out in the field with us.'

"I acted innocent and went about my business. The next morning we all assembled outside for revelry and roll call. Then I saw him. The First Sergeant walked up and stood right in front of me. He eyeballed me real hard. Sure enough! He was green!

"'Wiggins, I know that was you!' All his hair and skin was green. I couldn't resist, I put my hand over my mouth to keep from laughing out loud while his angry piercing eyes stared right back at me. 'Wiggins, I don't know how you did it, but I'm going to get you back!'

"A passed and the First Sergeant hadn't picked on me, in fact he didn't talk or say anything at all to me. By this time, I had already begun my specialized hand-to-hand combat training. One day I saw him talking to my hand-to-hand combat trainer. I didn't pay much attention to it and went about my business. They both talked for about forty-five minutes and then the First Sergeant left.

"Training was actually fun for me, and a week went by fast. that Saturday morning, right after breakfast, I was in the bunk house and noticed the First Sergeant walking up to my barracks.

"He opened the door and walked right up to me, 'Wiggins I want to talk to you outside.'

"Alright, I said to myself. I thought he wanted to fight. Man, this was the chance I was waiting for. We both walked outside the barracks. He turned around with a sudden move and stopped right in front of me.

"'Wiggins... me and you need to call a truce. I was talking to your Sergeant, the one who is training you. You saw me with him the other day. He told me you are in the top ten of the three hundred and fifty soldiers he is training. He said sometimes you come in first, sometimes third, and sometimes fourth, but you are one of his best. You,' he pointed at me, 'You ARE a soldier!' I noticed a faint smile on his face as he said, could we start over again?' and extended his hand. 'Shake my hand! Wiggins, I would be proud to have you at my side in combat any time.' And so we shook hands."

3

THE TRAINING CONTINUES

"The Art of Quickness"

"As my training continued I always sought out the harshest trainers because I knew they would train me well, the meaner the better. They were the ones who would show me how to survive.

"The selection process usually began like this. 'Soldier…!' (That was me), 'What are you doing in my squad?'

"We were expected to respond quickly and so I did. 'I want to learn everything you can teach me!'

"'You're too dumb to learn! You can't learn anything!'

"It went back and forth and finally, he would let me into his squad. As far as I was concerned, I was learning from the best.

"Each instructor had their own training techniques."

"Which one was the one that would make you dance?" Ray asked with a big smile.

"Our hand-to-hand combat instructor, he made us dance in order to build up our endurance. He would ask, 'Do you want to fight GOOD?'

"'Yes, sir!' we all answered.

"His expression was stern and serious. 'I'm going to teach you how to stay in shape. You will not only exercise and run, you will go dancing.' We all stood there in perplexed amusement and listened to the rest of our orders. 'Every Friday night, I will take you dancing, and you WILL dance. If there are no girls, you will still dance, by yourself, and you will dance every song! I don't care if you like, or don't like, the music! You W-i-l-l dance.'

"His motto was, *'If you can dance all night! You can fight all day.'* It is forever engrained in my mind.

"And so it was. Even after dancing all night, as soon as we got back to the barracks, he made us run five miles. Like clockwork, we danced every Friday or Saturday night. Then during the week, we trained in hand-to-hand combat techniques, rifle marksmanship, and in perfecting our skills disarming landmines. It was intense." I sat back in my chair, relaxed my shoulders, and took a long deep breath.

I looked at Ray and knew he wanted to ask another question.

Sure enough, "What other kind of training did you do, Dad?"

"Cartwheels" I answered. "They taught us cartwheels, it was part of perfecting our hand to hand combat skills. We practiced cartwheels every day for a solid week. We did cartwheels to the left and cartwheels to the right, all day long.

"First we did them using our hands, and then, without hands. For one week, we practiced each type of cartwheel all day. The following week, the cartwheel training intensified. The instructor had 3x5 colored cards. He took out a green card and held it in front of him a little higher than his shoulder. We had to approach him with a cartwheel and kick the green card with our left foot. If he pulled a red card, we had to kick it with our right foot. According to the colors he selected, we had to respond quickly with a cartwheel using the correct foot and kick the card in his hand.

"After a few days of perfecting this skill, the task became more challenging. It was my turn. He drew a red card. I flew into a cartwheel and as I was ready to kick the card with my right foot, he switched the card to green. In mid air, I had to make the adjustment and in a split second, 'POW' my toe hit the card on the money! As we all got better, the instructor switched out the 3x5 cards to smaller ones. Our hit had to be even more precise.

"By the end of the second week of doing this, we had perfected our skills. After this is when we began learning how to deliver a powerful kick. The instructor went and got a punching bag and held it to his chest.

"'Reach out Wiggins! Way out there! Touch the bag with the heel of your foot! When your foot reaches the bag, give it a push! Like a hard kick. Thrust your foot hard! Notice that when your foot makes contact with the bag, it pushes your body back. It is that backward momentum that is going to help bring you back onto your feet.'

"He held the punching bag and approached me, closer and closer, and from different angles. I had to kick the punching bag hard each time.

"As soon as the instructors were satisfied that we had learned a particular skill, they quickly shifted over to something else.

"'Jump up! Jump up in the air, as if you're going to throw a side kick. Jump as high as you can Wiggins, and kick this card.' He held it up high. I practiced it over and over. POW! Sometimes, as I kicked the card, I would fall down.

"'Don't worry, you'll learn,' the instructor said. 'Remember, the more you do it, the better you will be at it. Keep in mind, when you're going to kick someone, the momentum of that same kick is going to bring you back onto your feet.'

"I practiced over and over. I learned to control my foot and make a sharp hit.

"'Perfect!' I heard him yell out. He got the attention of everyone and said, 'I don't want to see anyone miss. If you do, I'm going to go right over there and kick you myself!'

"That day, we all passed, and at the end of those two weeks, this Sergeant made sure we were all skilled at kicking."

"What happened if someone couldn't learn what they were teaching you?"

"That was it for them. If at any time anyone was unable to learn a particular skill, bam! You were out! No second chances. It was at the end of those two weeks of intensive training when I realized that out of the three hundred and fifty soldiers that started the training, only two hundred were left."

"You mean one-hundred and fifty were eliminated?" Ray asked.

"Yes, after this part of the training," I answered, and nodded my head.

"What other type of things did you learn?"

"Well after this part of the training, we advanced to learning how to master our hand speed. We were given two small rocks. Then we were instructed to extend our arms straight out in front of us, palms facing down. We had to place the rocks on the backside of our hand, one rock behind the index finger nail, and the other rock on the knuckle of the same index finger. Then we had to fling the back side of our hand up, tossing the rocks up in the air, and try to catch each rock, one at a time, with the same hand before the rocks hit the ground. We started off with rocks,

50

and as soon as we perfected this skill, they exchanged the rocks for quarters. It was difficult, but we did it.

"When we mastered this skill with two quarters, they gave us another, then another, until finally we were practicing with five quarters. When I finally mastered catching all five quarters before they hit the ground, I asked the instructor, 'Why do you want me to catch all these quarters? How is this going to help me to fight?'

"'Wiggins,' he responded, 'With the hand speed you have just achieved, you can punch five people in the throat almost simultaneously! One right after another, and in a flash! It works, believe me!'"

"Dad," Ray said, "I bet that helped you when you had to rid the parks of those gangs in LA?"

"You better believe it. It was second nature to me, like when someone tosses you something and you reach out and catch it. That's the way it was for me. My reflexes were that good.

"Those instructors taught us so many skills, all with our feet and hands. I can still hear one of them saying, 'If you encounter an enemy while walking on a bridge, and he throws you a kick, you have to be able to counter with just one kick, and it has to be effective. You have to be able to not just kick him, but knock him off the bridge. It must be a powerful kick, a push, "un rampujón!"

"He taught us the art of quickness. 'Faster than an eagle, faster than a tiger, you got to be able to kick like a mule!'

"It didn't end there, the training continued."

"How long did all this training take Dad?"

"I lost track of time because it was so intense. I loved it; it was difficult but I learned things fast. We had to perfect our knife

51

fighting also. This one instructor lunged forward with his knife to demonstrate how to kill your enemy with a knife.

"'Get your knife! Don't just go like that to your enemy.' He demonstrated a regular stabbing move. 'When you're using a knife, you have to go in like this.' He lunged in swiftly but not forcefully. 'When you feel the knife make contact, slide it in slowly. Don't push it in, because if you hit a rib, the knife will stop. On the other hand, if you slide the knife in slowly, you will be able to go around the rib. Bend it a little bit-move it a tiny bit- and the knife will go around the bone.'

"For about a month, only on Fridays and Mondays, we trained with this instructor. I was real curious as to why he only worked with us those two days and so I asked, 'How come you don't work with us Monday and Tuesday, or Wednesday and Thursday?'

"Without hesitation he said, 'I work with you on Friday and Monday because on Friday, I teach you a new skill. I expect you to practice on your own Saturday and Sunday so that by Monday; I can see how well you've learned it.' I thought about it a bit. I didn't say anything out loud, but thought, 'Yep, it seems to work.'

"Right as we mastered one technique, immediately we proceeded on to another."

"How did you remember everything you were learning?" Ray asked.

"Well, since I was a little boy, I was strong and very coordinated. I also could learn things fast. I applied that same focus to my training. It was definitely challenging and difficult, but I mastered every lesson.

"One day I walked out to the field, they had set up a tennis ball machine. The machine was shooting out tennis balls at high speed. We each had to stand in front of this machine and deflect the balls with our hands, knees, feet, elbows. We couldn't use anything else. The machine spit out the balls fast and continuously. If a ball were to hit any other part of our body, we had to start over. This went on for several weeks until all of us could accurately deflect every single ball."

"Were you at Fort Sill all this time Dad?"

"Yes, until one day, out of the clear blue sky, we got orders to leave. Coincidently, a few days before this, we had been issued live ammo, hand grenades, and other supplies, basically everything we needed for a combat mission. Our orders said to pack up our gear. We had a flight waiting. We all got our gear together and boarded these small airplanes. Apparently, we were headed out to a base in Colorado. As soon as we landed in Colorado, we were transferred onto these larger airplanes that were waiting for us. From there, none of us knew our destination.

"I looked around the airplane; there was not one empty seat. The airplane was full of soldiers with their gear and their rifles. I looked out the small airplane window; below I saw nothing but ocean. In the distance, I noticed a formation of airplanes. It was unbelievable, airplane after airplane as far as I could see. There were hundreds of them, flying in the same direction. I didn't know where we were going. I sat there in silence, with only the loud roar of the airplane engine ringing in my ears.

"Pretty soon, my head was flooded with thoughts. The butt of my rifle firmly rested on my left foot and my two hands clinched the stock. I thought, 'Man... if I'm told to load this rifle, then what will I have to do?' I was prepared to do whatever they had trained me for. The combat skills I learned made me a very dangerous man.

"I looked around me and there were about forty to sixty soldiers packed into the airplane and absolutely no one was talking. I glanced into some of their faces and all I saw were blank stares. I imagined that all of them had the same anticipation I did. I sat quietly, just concentrating on the steady roar in my head from the engine noise. All of a sudden, I felt the airplane shift directions. For some reason, they turned all the airplanes around. We landed at Fort Dix New Jersey.

"As I stepped off the airplane, I looked in all directions. I couldn't believe it, there were thousands of soldiers! We were ordered to report to the barracks and find bunks, but there weren't enough bunks for all of us. The base was huge, and since there weren't enough bunks for everyone, orders were to sleep on the floor of any building we could find. Each of us was issued one blanket. There were no bunks and no heating. It was winter and the nights were very cold. Each morning we all lined up for chow, but the line was so long, that by the time we got done with breakfast, the line was already beginning for the next meal. Many of us were lucky if we got lunch or dinner."

"Dad," Ray suddenly asked, "Why were there so many soldiers there?"

"I'm not sure, but one thing is for sure, I know they hadn't planned for so many of us to be there at one time. After a few days though, some of the men began to get shipped out to other bases, including me."

"Where did you go?"

"I was sent to Fort Devens, Massachusetts, in a little town called Ayer. There was only one guy at Fort Devens that I recognized who had been with me at Fort Sill, and at Fort Dix.

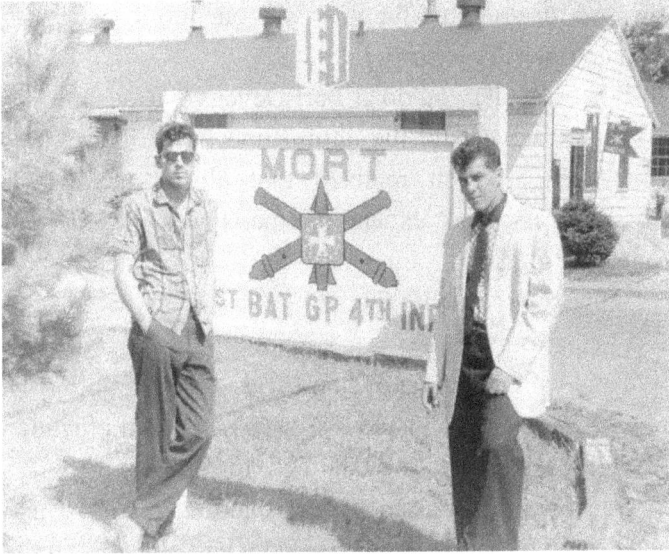

"As I recall, Fort Devens was about twenty miles from Boston. After talking to a few soldiers, I found out that everyone here was either airborne or special forces. As I said, when we arrived we had to sleep on the barrack floors. After a few days, we were brought sleeping cots, then iron beds, and finally mattresses and more blankets. We had a big wood and coal burning heater in the center of the barracks. We had plenty of coal and that's what we mostly burned. The winter nights were very cold, and so we always had someone posted on fire watch during the night.

"About a week or two later I was assigned to another part of the base; it was a 3.4 Mortar Company. I can't remember the battalion, but they put me in charge of radios and communications. Four of us were assigned to clean radios and to learn how to assemble and disassemble them. It was our job to get them ready for field maneuvers."

"What else did you do at Fort Devens?" Ray asked.

"That's what I did the entire time I was there, radios and communications. I soon realized that all the soldiers in my company were airborne, except for me. I was the only one that didn't have wings."

"Why were you with them?"

"I never found out."

"Time went by so fast when I was stationed at Fort Devens. We had to constantly clean and fix radios and then practice taking them out to the field and assigning them to soldiers.

"One Saturday morning I was getting ready to leave the base on a weekend pass, almost everyone had already left the base. There were about twenty of us soldiers still getting ready to leave. Right outside of our barracks, I saw a couple of officers approaching, and then they came inside.

"They stood there for a moment and then pointed at our direction and said, 'You, You, You, and You! You're going on a mission. Get all your gear!'"

"Were you one of the ones they picked?"

"Yeah," I answered Ray.

"Do you think it was planned?"

"I have no idea, but so much for our weekend passes!"

"I gathered all my gear, including some radios they asked us to bring, and boarded a waiting airplane. I had no idea why I was even here.

"About one hour into the flight, one of the officers snuck up behind us and shouted, 'This airplane has been hit by enemy fire!'

"Of course it really wasn't true. We all looked at each other figuring they were playing war games.

"One of the sergeants shouted, 'Our two pilots have already jumped out! All of you! You have to jump too!'

"Confused, I turned to the officer behind me and said, 'I don't have wings!'

"He answered, 'Son... TODAY... you get your wings.' He looked me straight in the eyes and said, 'You WILL jump!'

"I looked around and everyone else had already put on their parachute. I, too, quickly put mine on. The whole situation caught me by surprise."

"Were you scared?" Ray asked.

"Just a little bit at first, but I jumped anyway. I was one of the last to jump. I kept an eye on everyone below me to see when they were going to open their parachute, and I did the same thing. I hit the ground and did exactly what I had learned in boot camp. We had drilled over and over jumping off a high platform. We had to land rolling and land on our feet. When my feet hit the ground, I did just that, and nothing happened to me."

"Did you ever find out why they had picked you?"

"No, I just figured it was part of the training. Right after this, we were issued our orders. I was sent to Germany. It took us fourteen days by ship to finally get there.

4

THE COLD WAR ERA

"I Arrived in 1958"

I arrived in Germany in December of 1958, and left a year later, December of 1959. It was during the Cold War Era, but I didn't realize that until many years later. To my understanding, the Cold War was never really declared. It began in 1945, and it ended more or less, around October of 1990.

To understand the secrecy of the missions that I took part in, it is important to understand the political and geographical circumstances that existed between the United States, its allies and Germany after World War II. As World War II came to an end, the Soviet Union made it clear that they considered Eastern Europe, which included Bulgaria, Czechoslovakia, Hungary, Poland, and Romania, to be within their geographical influence. They were very adamant about not allowing Germany to ever regain any stability whatsoever. To ensure their objectives, the Soviet Union established the Soviet Alliance System in 1943, which enabled them to institute military and political control over these Eastern European countries (Bulgaria, Czechoslovakia, Hungary, Poland, and Romania).

After WWII, the allies, divided war torn Germany into four zones in order to expedite the reconstruction. The eventual result was American, British, and French zones, plus West Berlin; and a communist government in the Soviet zone of East Germany and East Berlin. Joseph Stalin had been leader of the Soviet Union for

30 years until his death in 1953. Before Stalin's death, Nikita Sergeyevich Khrushchev had risen from poverty to become the most powerful Russian in the Communist Party. Right after Stalin died, Khrushchev became their new leader. In May of 1955, three years before I was stationed in Germany, Khrushchev helped push through an agreement called the Warsaw Pact. Representatives of the Soviet Union which were Albania, Bulgaria, Czechoslovakia, Hungary, Poland, and Romania signed this pact. Immediately after this agreement, Soviet Union Red Army soldiers flooded Bulgaria, Czechoslovakia, Hungary, Poland, and Romania to create a "buffer zone" from possible future attacks to the Soviet Union from the West. The West, were the other three ally zones, the American, British, and French zones, plus West Berlin.

I was stationed in Germany from 1958 to 1959. I was a soldier in the Seventh Army. It was during the Soviet Union's Red Army border buildup of a "buffer zone." The Soviets had watch towers throughout the buffer zone and had also planted thousands of landmines. The Soviets were determined to prevent Germany from invading their country again. The Soviet Union had been invaded by Germany three times in the last 150 years. The Soviet Union, now known at the U.S.S.R. after the signing of the Warsaw Pact, was doing everything to prevent an invasion from ever happening again.

The training I had prepared me for my role in disarming landmines, among other things, in the "buffer zone." As a nineteen year old fresh to the military, I was unaware of the history making events that were taking place.

Figure 3 Frank Wiggins (center) Germany 1959, washing Howitzers

5

THE FIRST MISSION

"I Was Now Ready"

"When I first arrived in the town of Ansbach, Germany, I was amazed at what I saw. It was winter and there was lots of snow on the ground. I had never seen snow sleds pulled by horses. There were lots of them! Suddenly I had a big urge to take a ride on one of them. It was a great sight and I loved it! I thought it was the most beautiful place on earth. The people were different. The smells in the air were different. It felt so good that I was ready to re-enlist if it meant I would be able to spend more time here.

"I arrived on base and was assigned to a unit called the Eight Ball Platoon. I didn't know at the time that it was different. Every soldier there knew we were different from other platoon soldiers. There was an unspoken code of silence each of us had been trained in. Unlike other platoon soldiers who learned only one specialty within their tour of duty, we in the Eight Ball Platoon, had to learn each other's specialty. There were twelve of us in my squad, and in the coming weeks, we each learned to do everyone's specialty area.

"We had just settled into our barracks when orders came to report for training. It was time for field maneuvers. I packed my gear and heard we were headed for a place called Drafenville. I was vigilant of my surroundings. I noticed hundreds of Howitzers were being loaded on a train, and when the train was ready to head out, we followed in trucks. Training immediately began as soon as we arrived at our destination; it was intense. Our squad was assigned a Howitzer. Each Howitzer had twelve canoneers. We learned everything about that big gun.

We learned how to drive, shoot, man the fifty calibers, station the flags, set the timer on the round, as well as how to perform the maintenance. The entire training was fast paced and time went by quickly. Before I knew it, several weeks had passed, and we returned back to Ansbach.

"At first, being in Ansbach didn't seem so bad because I still had time to enjoy myself. We were not supposed to go out on the town at night, but I used to jump the base fence and wander the town taking in all the sights."

Ray almost startled me when he asked, "Dad, how did you talk to the people? Did they speak English?"

"No, some of the town kids taught me a few German words and I also remembered a little bit from my father, just enough.

"Our base had a unit that trained German shepherd's for military maneuvers and every day on my way back to our barracks from the chow hall, I came across this old dog that was tied to a long chain. He was an old retired military German shepherd. The dog was toothless, but still very mean. He wore a vest to keep him warm and on the vest were three stripes and a rocker to signify that during his service, this dog was a Sergeant. The vest on him also had metals of valor pinned to it. I could tell that in his prime, this German shepherd was a fierce dog.

"On my way back from the chow hall, I used to bring him leftover food. He especially loved it when I brought him meat balls because they were easy to chew. It didn't take long for the dog to trust me, but there were other soldiers who he really didn't like, especially the ones who enjoyed taunting and teasing him.

"These guys knew exactly how far the dog's chain could reach. They marked a line on the ground with their foot to indicate how far the dog could run before the chain yanked him back. The German shepherd took off running after them and when the dog reached the end of his chain, it fiercely jerked his whole body to a sudden stop. The guys would laugh. I couldn't stand to see the dog being teased. I didn't appreciate when anyone was taken advantage of, including animals.

"I decided the dog was going to have his day and so one afternoon, while no one was looking, I unchained him. The Shepherd stayed close to his dog house and no one could tell he was unchained. I looked around and found a good spot to sit; waiting to see what would happen when one of the guys started to tease him.

"As usual, a group of soldiers approached. Right away one of them started teasing the dog. The shepherd ran after the guy and sprinted past the drawn line. To the others surprise, he tackled him to the ground. It was funny because that old dog didn't have teeth, but he was mauling the soldier with his gums. The soldier's uniform was drenched with saliva from the dog's toothless drooling. The Shepherd's legs were still powerful, and he had the soldier pinned to the ground. It was so funny, the guy was shouting for help and attempting to scramble to his feet but couldn't. He finally managed to get away and the dog returned back to his dog house as if nothing had happened. The shepherd was smart; he waited for another unaware soldier to tease him.

"All afternoon the same thing happened over and over again. I laughed so hard watching the whole thing. Pretty soon everyone who had been mauled waited with me while their unsuspecting friends encountered the same fate. I laughed so hard that day; and after this, nobody ever teased the dog again."

"Dad," Ray asked, "How long were you in Germany before you went out on your first mission?"

"Let's see, I left Fort Devens around Christmas, and it took 14 days by ship to get there. I spent New Year's on ship and by the time we arrived in Germany, it was already the first week of January 1959. We trained intensely up to July and it was after that. I was there around seven months before I went on a mission. All the training kept me pretty busy, but it went by real fast."

"Did you know you were training for these missions?"

"No, all I knew is that I was training for combat.

"Then one day during training, this one Sergeant approached a group of us and said, 'Get ready, we're going to have a shooting contest, to find out who's the best shot.'

"I thought to myself, 'Why do they need to know who can shoot the best, they already have our qualification records.' I suspected we were in for some war games.

"Since a very young age, my brothers taught me not to trust easily, my senses quickly heightened."

"How many of you were asked to go?"

"Only a handful, we were motioned to board a couple of jeeps that were waiting for us. We hopped in, and off they drove. About an hour later, we reached what I thought was our destination. Everyone jumped off. I looked around for the open range targets, but didn't see any. All of a sudden, two more jeeps arrived, and we were motioned to get in."

"I bet that sure made you more suspicious."

"It sure did! A short time later, we arrived at a big warehouse way outside of town. The building was huge. Inside, the place was set up as an indoor firing range. We were instructed to shoot with twenty-two peep sights."

"Why twenty-two's? Isn't that a pretty small rifle for combat?"

"We only used them to simulate firing with a larger caliber rifle inside the building. Each of us fired a couple of rounds and it didn't take long before we all perfected hitting our targets. When that was done, the instructors wheeled in these huge fans. They positioned the fans where they could blow across the firing range."

"Why did they do that?"

"It was to simulate wind conditions. They taught us how to compensate for wind factor. The instructors were very pleased with my marksmanship skills, and I was very happy about that. I had exceptional vision, *'If I could see it, I could hit it!'*

"After our practice that day, I was given a three day pass to use when we got back to base."

"Did any of the other guys get a pass?"

"I don't know, probably."

"Where did you go on your pass?"

"I went to town and had a good time. It felt so good to get away from the base.

"A few days later, again, I was taken for some more marksmanship training.

"I had just returned to base when from the corner of my eye, I saw a couple of officers approaching, 'Wiggins, get your gear, we're taking you to a shooting competition.'

"I thought, 'Wow, I guess I did so well that I'm going on a special trip.'"

"Where was the shooting competition?"

"I heard them say Nuremberg, a town about twenty-five miles from base. Again, just a few of us guys were chosen and I met up with them at waiting jeeps. But just as we were about to leave, they told me my orders were changed. They took the other guys and left me there. I was mad and felt deceived."

"I bet you were pissed off!"

"I was, and I was also disappointed! I couldn't understand why they did that. Another jeep arrived that was for me, so instead of going to a shooting competition, I was taken to a place outside of Nuremberg."

"Were you by yourself?" Ray asked

"No, there were two jeeps and they had picked up a few other soldiers on the way, none of whom I had ever met.

"The jeeps drove late into the night until we arrived at a place where we were supposed to bed down for the night. It was a small house with a shed like building next to it.

"'Take off your name tags,' one of the officers said, 'and from now on, you're not to talk to one other.' I did as told, but I stayed alert.

"By this time I was suspicious of everyone. I lay still in my sleeping bag, and for the first time since arriving in Germany, I had second thoughts of being there. I really hated being deceived and I made up my mind that I should absolutely not trust anyone. I lay there sleepless, trying to figure out all the possible reasons why I was with this particular group of soldiers. To my recollection, I had never trained with these guys. So why was I with them? I was the runt of the bunch. The rest looked like ex-football players. When I finally closed my eyes, all I could think of was home.

"Early the next morning we were ordered to pack our gear from a storage bunker next to the house. It was not our usual gear, we packed snow suits, jackets, boots and live ammo. No one was saying much except for the officers. I overheard them saying we were headed toward the East German border.

"My suspicions heightened, 'Looks like every man for himself!'

"We climbed into the back of two big trucks and drove all night. Early in the morning the trucks came to an abrupt stop. I overheard one of the officers in the truck say we were about a mile and half from the East German border. Everyone jumped out and stood around waiting for orders.

"Then one of the officers walked toward us, he stopped right in front of me. 'This here is a practice run! We're headed to a location loaded with landmines.' He looked at me, 'When we reach our destination, I want you to clear a ten kilometer path, one over and one back. Clear the first path and then wait for us to reach you. We'll decide then, when we're coming back. Do you understand?'

"He looked at me as if I didn't hear him. 'That's all you're supposed to do!'

"'Yes sir!' I answered, 'Piece of Cake!' I thought, 'I've been trained to do this.'

"Right before I took off to do my job, I called the squad together and started showing them how to read the symbols I was about to mark the path with. They needed to read my markings in order to cross safely. Otherwise, they might step on a landmine I hadn't removed.

"Just as I got started, a First Lieutenant interrupted me, 'I'm the only one that calls my squad together, and I'm the one who's going to show them how to get across!'

"'Okay,' I told him, 'Then you're the one that can show them how to read my markings when you're following my path tonight!'

"I stood up and started gathering my gear. The First Lieutenant remained quiet for a little while.

"He looked at his men, and then at me. 'Carry on soldier. Show everyone the markings.'

"I squatted down and with my finger, drew markings on the dirt that indicated different signals. For instance, I drew symbols that indicated when to turn, when to go straight, approximately how many yards to proceed, and to alert them if there were guards up ahead. 'Remember these markings,' I said, 'This is how you're going to make it safe across this field without getting blown up. When I draw a straight line that means you have a two foot width of a safety area. Don't put your hands, arms, or legs out further than those two feet!'

"It took me about twenty minutes to explain all the shorthand markings I had been taught by my instructor at Fort Sill.

"One of the soldiers asked, 'What if I can't remember them?'

"I answered him, 'If you can't remember them, make sure to stay behind a guy who can.'

"'Can you show them to us one more time?' Another guy asked.

"And so I did. When I was done explaining one more time, I told them, 'Wait for me until nightfall or until I give you a signal to cross.'

"One of the soldiers asked 'Why do we have to stay behind and wait, why can't we just walk behind you now?'

"'You might get spotted by the guard tower and shot. There are twenty-one of us. If we all head out at the same time, our chances of getting spotted are twenty-one times more likely than just one guy crawling on the ground.'

"The First Lieutenant confirmed my answer, 'He's right.'"

I was so caught up thinking about the events of that first mission that I almost forgot Ray was sitting across from me. His voice brought me back to the present, "Dad was this the first time you were clearing a minefield by yourself?"

"Yeah, but I was up for it. As soon as I finished explaining to them my markings, I headed out and the others remained behind, waiting for nightfall.

"Should I keep going?" I asked Ray, "Or should we save the rest for tomorrow."

"No, let's keep going, I might have to work tomorrow," Ray answered.

"When I reached the landmine area, I quickly scanned the terrain and gathered branches, twigs, grass and whatever the surrounding had in order to camouflage my presence."

"Could you see the landmines?"

"Heck, when I looked out, I could see all of them! They stuck up like big old sore thumbs! I dug them out real quick and deactivated them by carefully slipping the safety pins back in. I placed each one safely aside on the perimeter of the path I was clearing. It seemed like only an hour had passed when I finished. I crawled over to a distant tree and slowly raised my hand to signal our spotter that I was done. It was my turn to rest. Even though I was done, they still had to wait about two hours, until dusk, to head over. I found a comfortable spot under some bushes and waited.

"Finally they arrived. A couple of the guys quietly came over to me and shook my hand. One of guys whispered, 'Good markings, that's the fastest we've ever crossed.' Even the First Lieutenant shook my hand and nudged my shoulder with his. Now that really surprised me!

"'Take us farther in,' the First Lieutenant told me.

"I continued to clear landmines as I led them across about one and a half kilometers into East German territory. When I looked back, one of the officers motioned for me to stop. I thought, 'Mission accomplished looks like we're going back.'

"When I turned around, the Second Lieutenant came up close to me and said, 'We shouldn't go back the same way we came, let's go back on a different path.'

"This Lieutenant hadn't said anything up until now. I looked at him and thought, 'This guy really wants to see what I can do.'

"'Can you clear a path at night?'

"Without hesitation I answered, "Yes sir," and started working on it. The squad dispersed under brush cover and waited for me to signal them.

"I looked around and right away found a good place to clear the return path. I could still see the ground and the landmines were easy to detect. The smell of damp dirt filled my nose as I crawled from place to place. It was cold and there was still a light film of snow that hadn't melted during the day. I figured we might be getting some more snow pretty soon so I wanted to hurry.

"I was fast and cleared the path in nothing flat. 'I'm done!' I whispered to the Lieutenant upon my return.

"'No!' he said. 'I wanted you to clear it in the dark.'

"I looked at him suspiciously and thought 'these guys are really testing me.'

"I said to him, 'There's nothing wrong with this one, but if you don't want it, I can clear another one.'

"'Do you think you can clear it at night?'

"'Yes.' I immediately replied, 'But now it's really dark and it's going to take me all night.'

"'Okay,' replied the Second Lieutenant, 'We'll wait over here.'

"I had only a bayonet to dig out the landmines and no light whatsoever, so it did take me all night. I was only a third of the way across to our return destination when finally some rays of light from the early dawn lit the ground. I glanced across the field, 'Oh yeah' I easily detected the rest of the land mines. Swoop! I cleared the rest of the field in nothing flat. I doubled back and from a distance, I motioned with my hand, 'Ok, it's clear.' Everyone came across."

"So that was your first mission?" Ray asked.

"Yes, that was my first mission."

"How long were you gone?"

"It had been three weeks since I had left for the so called "shooting competition," and now we were finally returning to Ansbach.

"In those short three weeks that I was gone, it seemed like the town had changed. Some of the snow had melted and lots of people were outside enjoying the good weather. For the first time I noticed the big beautiful red cobblestones in the streets that had been covered with snow. At night I walked around the festive streets. I was amazed of all the carnivals throughout the town. I had no idea that after the next four months, my life would never be the same again."

Figure 4a - Seventh Army Insignia

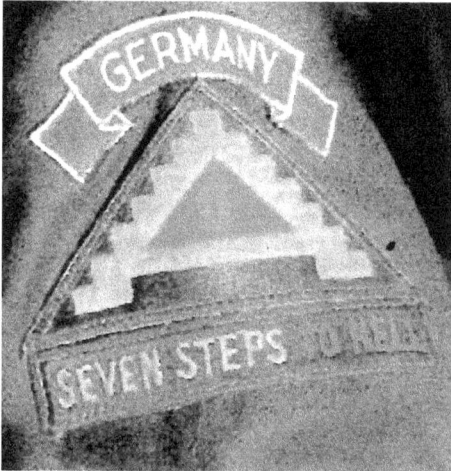
Figure 4b -Unofficial Seventh Army Patch worn by soldiers.

6

SECOND AND THIRD MISSIONS

"What is Freedom?"

"My second mission was very much like the first, just another trial run. But the third mission, that one was a little tougher because we had to take these big radios across the border.

"Usually I didn't have to carry anything because that was the job of other soldiers. I was the point man, my job was to clear mine fields. I was given a map and it was up to me to guide the squad to the destination marked on that map. I was good at reading maps with a compass and that was probably because I was good with numbers. Even as a young boy I was good with numbers."

Ray was quiet, and looked intently at my face, "Did you say that on the third mission, they were only carrying batteries and radios? What kind of radios were they?"

I grinned as I described them to Ray, "When I say radios, I don't mean little radios like we have now. They were these big bulky things that weighed about thirty-five pounds each."

"Dad, do you remember what the weather was like on that day?"

I slowly slipped back in time. It sure helped that Ray was there to ask me questions, slowly I was remembering more of the many memories I had blocked out over the years because of the guilt of my last mission. I felt it was now time to tell my story. Maybe if other veterans read it, it could help them with some of their own PTSD. My wife Lenora and family had been trying to help me write these stories many times over the past fifteen years, but it was too difficult. Something would always come up and I would forget about it. I probably wouldn't be doing this right now if it were not for Ray.

Ray noticed I was deep in thought and I forced myself to stay focused on his question. "The weather was still changing during that time of the year. I remember it was wet, and I could smell the shrubs and pine trees around me. It smelled fresh."

"About how many soldiers were with you on this mission?"

"Besides me, there were about thirteen. Some had no rank on their uniforms so I couldn't tell who they were or why they were with us. Everything was always very secretive and I never knew any details, and no one ever called anyone by their name. There were two things I could count on, one was that on every mission, I was called "Sergeant," and the other was that whenever we got within one or two kilometers into enemy territory, I was always signaled to stay back."

"Stay back where?" Ray asked.

"Stay behind. They didn't want me to go with them. The reason was that they didn't want anything to happen to me. If something happened, if I got shot, then they wouldn't have anyone trained to clear a path back through the mine field for them. On this mission, I stayed back, but kept an eye on them until the very end. Right before they disappeared on the other side, they stopped. I saw all of them quickly change into civilian clothes and stuff their combat uniforms into their packs."

"Why do you think they changed into civilian clothes?"

"At the time I didn't think anything of it because I was never told much of anything. They probably wanted to blend in with the civilians, with the German people."

"So what did you do while they were gone?"

"I worked every single second. I had lots of time and didn't want to get bored. First, I cleared a return path for us. I had to be careful not to be spotted by the Russian Guard Towers, so I had to crawl on my stomach and inch along the shrubs while clearing the path of land mines.

"I was trained to prepare for anything and be prepared for every possible scenario. If our guys got spotted and the enemy came chasing after us, I had to be ready to get them back safely. When I was done, I found a safe place to hide inside a gully surrounded by bushes and trees, and then waited. I kept a constant look out with my M1. The MI rifle has a powerful zoom and I kept an eye on the patrols which were passing every two hours. I didn't want to be spotted."

"How long did you wait?"

"Four days. Finally, I saw them coming. I spotted some movement. I counted twelve people. They were dressed in civilian clothes and making their way toward me. It was close to dusk, but I could still see clearly. Several of the people were wearing combat uniforms under their civilian clothes.

"Traveling with the squad were an older man, a woman and two kids. There were also three other people. Two of them were men about forty to forty-five years old, and a woman who looked about fifty. Thirteen people left, twelve people were returning, and half of them different. Who knows if the people left behind were actually soldiers?"

"What happened when they reached you?"

"Right away I led them back to camp. It took several days because we rested and slept during the day then traveled quietly at night. With so many people traveling, it was too easy to be spotted by the enemy patrols in the guard towers.

"When we rested, I kept my distance from the rest of the group. My orders were not to associate or talk to the civilians. It was hard to ignore them because they were very curious and they kept asking me questions."

"What kind of questions?" Ray asked.

"Mostly about freedom. I remember sensing they were no ordinary people because they appeared to be well educated. They must have had something we wanted, something important."

"Did you talk to them?" Ray asked.

"I tried not to. It wasn't my business to ask questions. The older man and woman spoke fluent English but their kids didn't. The kids were afraid and they kept their distance from everyone.

"To me it was strange; they asked things like, 'What is it like to be free?' I could see fear in their eyes. 'We're going to the United States and we don't know what it is to be free. Can we go from one city to another without telling somebody? Do we need a Visa to travel?' They were persistent and finally I answered all their questions as best as I could.

"There was a waiting truck when we got back to our base camp and everyone got in. I sat in the back of the truck and could overhear their conversation. I understood a little German, but they didn't know."

Ray looked at me surprised, "I don't think I remember you ever saying you knew how to speak German."

"I knew just enough to communicate a little."

"Where did you learn it?"

"My mother taught me. Remember I told you she spoke about five different languages."

"Did your father speak German?"

"Sometimes, from what I know, my father didn't speak English until he was about forty years old, he mostly spoke Spanish. He spoke a little German, but that was only to my mom when he didn't want us to know what they were saying. He also spoke a little Navajo and Tewa."

"What was your dad, I mean, what nationality was he?"

"I don't know that much about my dad. My mom said she thought he was part Indian and part German. My father's birth name was Benedito Wiggins. He was born in Cuba, New Mexico. His father's name was Pablo Wiggins and his mother's name was Elvira Sanchez. My mother told me my Dad's father was a very wealthy man in Cuba.

"The story I was told was that my grandfather, Pablo Wiggins, was one of three brothers who were on a ship coming from Germany in the early 1800's, and they decided to jump ship. One migrated to Mexico, another to Texas, and Pablo came to reside in New Mexico.

"He married and had a family but he also had affairs with other women. While married to his wife, he had two illegitimate boys with two different women. One of the boys was my father, Benedito.

"When the first boy, Isidor, was born, my grandfather sent him to be raised by a family in Farmington and paid the family well to do that.

"When my father, Benedito, was born, his mother, Elvira Sanchez raised him until her death. She died at a very young age. When she died, Pablo Wiggins paid another family, the Gomez family, to raise him. The Gomez family lived in Coyote a small town just outside of Cuba. From what my mother told me, he had a very rough life after his mother died.

"My father was twelve years old when his father, Pablo, showed up out of nowhere. Benedito, my father, thought his last name was Gomez until his father Pablo showed up.

"He told him, 'I am your father! You are not a Gomez or a Sanchez! You are a Wiggins!'"

Ray was almost on the edge of his chair, "I don't remember you ever telling us that before."

"Your mother is the one who remembered this, she just reminded me of it not too long ago." I continued, "My mother said that when my grandfather Pablo's wife died, he brought my Dad's half brother, Isidor, back from Farmington.

"I'm not sure exactly how it happened, but when my Dad was seventeen, he met his half brother, Isidor. A little after that my Dad also met his four half sisters from his father's deceased wife. My father, Benedito, was a very strict man. He had a mean streak. He lived a very rough life growing up."

I couldn't remember how I got started on this story and asked Ray, "How did I get started on this subject?"

"I think it was when I asked you how you knew German."

"Oh yeah," I said and as soon as I said that, I drifted into another memory. Ray knew I was deep in thought, and didn't say anything. I was remembering the last time I spoke German. It was in 1995. That was the year I had a big flashback and lost a lot of my memory. I blacked out for thirteen hours and still don't know what happened during that time. For about a week after this flashback, I kept having other smaller ones, every few hours. I was very sick and didn't know it.

I remember driving myself to the VA Hospital in Albuquerque and then being admitted to Ward Seven by my doctor. Ward Seven is the Detoxification, Alcohol, and Drug Abuse Program Unit of the VA. That turned out to be another nightmare I didn't need.

First the hospital couldn't find my military records and so I gave them my original DD214 (Army discharge paper) for verification. Then the hospital administration accused me of making it up. They said they needed to investigate the authenticity of my DD214 and service in the United States Army, and also to prove my service in Germany. There was an APO number on the DD214 which proved I was overseas.

The VA then lost my original DD214 but luckily, at the urging of a VFW advocate, I had made a notarized copy for my files just months before. In the meantime, while the VA was investigating my DD214, I was admitted.

While in Ward Seven, I felt like I was being interrogated. One time in particular they asked me if I could speak German and I said, "No, I can't." I really couldn't remember speaking German at all.

The following day, the same staff members were there in my ward and this one woman came up to me and said "Begats, Frank, (hello, Frank). You sprenchen sic Deutsch?" (Do you speak German?) And I said "Nein, Ich spreche Kein Deutsch. (No, I don't speak German) Ech verstche nur ein wenig," (I understand only a little bit). She excitedly clapped her hands and left quickly. I still don't know how I remembered that.

I almost forgot Ray was in the room with me. I was back in time for just a few minutes, but it seemed like hours.

"Dad, you seemed to learn things real fast, is that because of your photographic memory?"

"Yes, I suppose so."

"So when did you know you had a photographic memory?"

"I think it was when I was about seven years old, at the time, we were living in San Jose, California. After a conversation with my mother, I realized I could remember lots of things most people couldn't. Before that, I just thought everyone was like me. I guess I took after my mother, Frances Losana Sanchez Wiggins; your grandmother was a linguist and could speak five languages."

"How did she learn so many languages?" Ray asked.

"My mother had gone to school to become a teacher. Her first job out of college was teaching in a one room school house in the Jemez Mountains of New Mexico. When in college, she had to take language courses. There were lots of Native American kids in the classroom and she wanted to learn their language to help them."

"Where was my grandmother born?" Ray asked.

"In Tularosa, New Mexico, my mom soon realized that what most people learned in eight months, she learned in one month. When she discovered this, she started learning other languages. We lived in Jemez until I was about four years old and then moved to San Jose, California, there, she got a job as a teacher. One day some people came to her school looking for people who could speak multiple languages because they needed translators in the court house and that's when she changed jobs.

"Because of her language fluency, my mother was able to assist the Cubans, Puerto Ricans, Frenchmen, Germans and Samoan people as they pleaded their cases in court. At the time, I was only four years old and too young for my mother to leave me at home alone, so she took me to work with her, at court. I learned a lot just by listening and also by her teaching me at home. By the time I was nine years old, I could understand French, German, and Spanish."

"How did you know for sure you had a photographic memory?"

Ray was very curious how I came to this realization. Growing up, things always came easy for him too. Ray graduated from high school when he was only sixteen. My youngest daughter, Jaime, started talking when she was only six months old. I was getting tired, but forced myself to continue explaining.

"Like I said, I really didn't realize I could learn things faster than other people, I thought it was normal. Then, when I was seven and half years old, I realized I was different. At the time, we lived in a house right behind Hill View Airport in San Jose, and behind the airport, were mountains, the east foothills. Twenty miles up, was Mt. Hamilton peak, and on top of it, was the James Lick Observatory. My friends and I used to go walking in the mountains all the time. This one time we walked all the way up the mountain and arrived at the Observatory. We got there just in time for one of the tours and decided to go in."

"Was it the first time you had been there?"

"Yes. The tour was real interesting and then when it was over and we were leaving, this one man, he must of worked there, asked me something about the stars and I guess my response must have impressed him. I don't remember what I said, but it must have interested him.

"He bent down to look at me and without an expression asked, 'Well, son, do you remember everything I talked about today?'

"And I immediately said 'Yes!'

"He raised his eyebrows, 'Really? Tell me a few things you remember.'

"I told him everything I remembered. About the stars, universe, the galaxies, everything in detail, that was talked about on the whole tour.

"He seemed very surprised and then said 'Come by next Sunday, I want to show you something.'

"I wanted to see what he was going to show me. The following Sunday, I persuaded my brother Willie to give me a ride to the Observatory."

"How old was your brother Willie?" Ray asked.

"Let's see, Willie is about seven years older than me… He must have been about fourteen, he was already driving."

"What happened when you got there?"

"I opened the big doors of the observatory and a bunch of people were standing around the big telescope. The man who had invited me came over and guided me over to all those people.

"He said, 'This is the kid I told you about.'

"From that day on, I visited the observatory frequently. I didn't even miss hanging out with friends my age anymore. Whether it was a Friday, Saturday, or Sunday, I spent hours with these people looking through the telescope. They would even take turns picking me up at my house. I was so good with numbers that I could remember lots of things about the constellations and how to locate stars. They would even ask me my opinion and treat me like an adult. They seemed to really enjoy my company and I liked spending time looking at the stars and galaxies."

"How long did you do that for?" Ray asked.

"I did that practically every weekend from the time I was seven and half until I was thirteen."

"Wow! That was a long time Dad. Why did you stop?"

"It just so happened that one day I was fixing my room in the garage, I stepped up on top of a stool and it tipped over with me on it. I hit the back of my head so hard that from that moment on, I lost memory of everything. I mean everything......of my friends, my family, everything!"

"You mean, just like that?" Ray asked in disbelief.

"Yes, I couldn't remember anything from one day to another! It was bad. For a long time, I couldn't even remember what my mother looked like from one day to another. Each day I would come home from school and run to her like an excited little kid. I would tell her everything I had learned that day while looking deep into her eyes. I was memorizing the contours of her face as we talked. I was so afraid I wouldn't be able to find my mother because I couldn't remember what she looked like from one day to another, it was awful."

"How long did that last?"

"About a year, I finally regained a lot of my memory and began learning things quickly again, but only things that interested me. For some reason, I lost interest in the stars and never went back to the observatory." I glanced at Ray, "I now know that this ability, having a photographic memory, made learning easy for me, and I learned a lot of things."

"Dad, do you think the military knew you had that ability?"

"I'm sure they did! That's probably why they trained me in so many things."

I was tired; I hadn't remembered that much in a longtime. Since the flashback, I seemed to be in a cloud most of the time and the memory of these events, seemed like a whole lifetime ago. I realized I had had a unique gift. I took a deep breath; it had been a long day.

I looked at my son and said, "Ray, I'm tired."

"Ok Dad."

7

FOURTH MISSION

"Changed Forever"

"How are you feeling today?" Ray said, greeting me with a smile. "Do you feel ready to talk about the fourth mission?"

"Yes, I'm ready."

"How long did you say you were gone on that third mission?"

"It must have been somewhere between nine to thirteen days before we returned back to our base."

"How did the fourth mission start?"

I thought for a bit, "That one was one of the toughest for me."

"What made that one so hard?" Ray asked.

I looked at him and lowered my head thinking back to the details of that day, "It was the first time I had to kill." Immediately after saying that, I flashed back to mid September of 1959.

"It was fall and the weather was already getting cold. There were sporadic snow showers and the snow was starting to stick to the ground. It had been a little over a week since I had returned from my third mission.

"After lunch, we all lined up to get our orders for the day and when it was my turn, the Sergeant yells out, 'Wiggins, Trash Detail!'

"Hmm, I knew instantly this was not an ordinary trash detail, it was my prompt, my secret dispatch code for another mission. I reported to battalion headquarters for my orders and as far as I knew, not even my immediate chain of command knew where I was taken when the jeep arrived to pick me up for 'Trash Detail.'"

"Where do you think your orders were coming from?"

"I don't know. It must have been covered up pretty good. Even though my immediate officers never asked any questions when I returned from "trash detail," the other soldiers did. I couldn't tell anyone where I had been. Eventually the other soldiers began to treat me different. Pretty soon, I felt like an outcast and it got steadily worse. No one ever saw where I was doing trash detail. They were jealous, they thought I was getting gravy jobs and assumed I was having fun and they weren't."

Ray noticed I was looking a little tired. "Dad, do you want to take a break?"

"No, that's alright. Where was I?"

"The Fourth Mission," Ray quickly responded.

"Oh, yeah, that particular day I got my orders and waited for my ride. I never knew if it was going to be a jeep or truck. I was learning to expect the unexpected. A jeep arrived and along the way we picked up a few more soldiers, as usual, we didn't know each other. We arrived at our meeting point, the post office. From there, I boarded one of several trucks and headed to Nuremburg."

"How far was Nuremburg from Ansbach?"

"It was about twenty-five miles southwest of Ansbach. When we got to Nuremburg, the trucks backed up to a supply bunker and while the trucks loaded their supplies, we too went inside to pack everything we might need for this mission. This was becoming routine for me. I never took much food, just candy bars and beef jerky. I did this for a purpose, and that was to make room in my packs for more ammo. I went to grab the ammo clips and noticed some APB's."

"APB's?"

"Yeah," I answered Ray. "At that time the military was experimenting with Teflon-coated bullets, they were called Armor-Piercing Bullets, APB's."

Ray seemed surprised, "I didn't know they had those back then?"

"Yeah, they were new. The military discovered that if a bullet was coated with Teflon, it could go right through a bullet proof jacket, even steel pot helmets. My mind was always thinking of possibilities and so right away I figured, 'Well, if one single bullet has the capability of penetrating a steel pot helmet, then it could penetrate several bodies at one time.'"

"How's that," Ray asked.

"Well, when soldiers line up right next to one another in formation, they become a perfect target. If you were a sharp shooter and fired with an APB, the bullet could penetrate two to three of them at once."

"IF you were LUCKY," Ray said laughing.

"I WAS!" I said with a grin. "Anyway, this was the first time APB's were available to us, so I packed them too. In fact, I took eight clips and put them on my cartridge belt, I also stuffed seventy rounds in my side and back pockets. I never put any ammunition in my front pockets."

"Why?" Ray asked.

"Because it interfered with crawling on my stomach as I cleared mine fields."

"That makes sense."

"I was always thinking ahead. If I was told to take five hand grenades, I took twenty, and that kind of thinking got me out alive. *'Better to have it and not need it, rather than not take it and need it!'* That's the advice my sergeant at Fort Sill had given me and I lived by it."

"What happened next?"

"We drove all night and part of the next day before arriving at our destination. It was a small German house that had been converted into our operation headquarters. Everyone went inside. Most of the men went inside to find a place to sleep. Traveling with us was a Lieutenant, Captain, Sergeant and Warrant Officer, who went to another room to meet with the Colonel."

"How many of you were there?" Ray asked.

"About thirteen, this included the Colonel who had met us there. I never could sleep in late and so I was up early the following day. I waited anxiously for the others to wake up. Finally, around nine o'clock, the men gathered for their assignments. Immediately I began checking out the terrain and looking for the best spots to start clearing a path. We were close to the German border and the zone was littered with mines. The Russians didn't want anyone crossing over into East Germany, and they also didn't want any East Germans escaping into West Germany, our side.

"Each soldier got their orders and immediately searched for a comfortable place to spread their ponchos. Everyone settled in and waited for nightfall. During my first missions, I was briefed on what to expect.

"No soldier ever called anyone by name and no one ever knew their real rank. I was always given an armband displaying Sergeant Stripes. We never knew each other's assignments, and no one talked to one another. My guess was, the less each soldier knew about each other or about what we were doing there, the less we could tell, in case we got caught.

"While they rested, I set out to scout the area and do my work. I saw a Russian guard tower in the far distance, so quietly, I crawled on my stomach disarming the landmines throughout the path I was creating. I finished before nightfall and when it got dark enough, I signaled the squad to cross.

"As soon as they crossed over, I got busy creating another path, a safe exit route for their return. My plan was to clear a path half mile into enemy territory."

"About how many yards is that?" Ray asked.

"About 800 yards, but it seems like five miles when you're crawling on your belly. When I had finished, the shape of the two paths resembled a horse shoe.

"My job was always twofold; as I uncovered an enemy landmine, I disarmed it, removed it carefully, and hid it on the side of the trail I was clearing. I hid them in stacks of five and ten then covered them with dirt. When I was half way through the mine field, I didn't bother to hide them anymore. When I reached the end of the trail, I doubled back and hauled them all out quickly. I was good at my job; I had disarmed more than a hundred landmines and these I now set out to re-arm into booby traps.

"I worked into the night with little rest and the following morning, continued working around the patrols as they passed my area every few hours. Quietly, I worked feverishly between their rounds. It took me three days to finish."

"How did you know where to put the booby traps?"

"I had a method. I set the booby traps in clusters of five, ten, and fifteen. If I didn't want the enemy to go in a certain direction, I positioned booby traps so they could easily be seen. I knew they would walk away from that area and into an area in which I set a trap.

"My favorite strategy was positioning booby traps in a V-shaped pattern. The length of each arm of the 'V,' was twenty-five feet and the distance across the opening, was also twenty-five feet. To the unsuspecting eye, the area of the 'V' appeared clear and safe. I fooled the enemy into walking about twenty feet into the 'V,' by the time their point man discovered it was a trap, it was too late, and his foot was on top of a mine cluster. To this cluster, I had attached a thin nylon line and connected it to each of the other mines I planted along the 'V,' arms. I buried nine clusters on one side and ten on the other side. Each cluster was set to go off four seconds apart. Usually, when the point man stepped on the inside cluster, the whole squad was already inside the trap. Boom! Boom! Boom! A chain of lethal landmines exploded around them. Shrapnel scattered all over the place and usually no one survived."

"How long did you say it took you to finish setting all those booby traps?"

"Three days, and by the time I finished, I was exhausted. I looked for a comfortable place to rest and found one about a hundred yards beyond the Russian guard patrols. From there, I could see anyone approaching.

"I waited all day and into the late afternoon. All of a sudden, I heard men coming. It was our men. They were deep in enemy territory and rushing through the trees in my direction. They were in a big hurry. I sensed something bad had happened so I headed toward them.

"'What happened?' I asked them, when I got there.

"One of the officers was in a panic and answered, 'they're coming, two trucks, we spotted them, and they're coming in our direction!' He wanted to hurry up and return back across the border.' I turned toward the rest of the squad who was following behind him a short distance away. Stop, I signed with my hand.

"Crouching down, I whispered to the Lieutenant, 'The guards in front of us cross every two hours and they're half an hour into their patrol. We have enough time to cross, but I wouldn't advise it. I pointed to the guard towers up ahead, 'They can easily spot us in the daylight. We have to watch the guards until they complete one more patrol and then we can cross, and by then, it'll be dark.'

"'I'm in charge!' the Lieutenant snapped. He didn't understand that what I was saying was just common sense. Arrogantly he answered, 'If I want, I can take us across right now!'

"I looked at him and didn't want to argue. 'Then I'll see you in the next life,' I said. Turning my back at him, I muttered, 'Or you can wait.'

"He knew I was right. It would be suicide to attempt crossing all the men in daylight. He thought about what I had said and reluctantly ordered the men to wait. The squad quietly scattered and hid in the surrounding brush.

"The Lieutenant crawled over to where I was, 'They spotted us!' His eyes kept looking in the direction they had just come from. 'I want you to go back where we saw the trucks and find them. When you do, kill them all!' It was obvious he wanted to intimidate me. Coldly he added, 'It's now YOUR job Sergeant, to make sure they can't find or identify any of us! Understand! *If you can't kill them all, then don't bother coming back!'*

"The Lieutenant seemed pissed off at his predicament."

"Why was he mad at you, Dad?"

"He hated the fact that since he was sending me to go find the trucks and kill the enemy, he now was responsible to take the men back. It was he who had to wait and determine when it was safe to cross, and hopefully not get them all blown up."

"Why would that bother him so much?"

"Because I was the one who usually did that, I could do it fast and easy. So now I had to show the Lieutenant and Sergeant real quick how to read the markings I had drawn on the return path, and so I gave them a quick lesson."

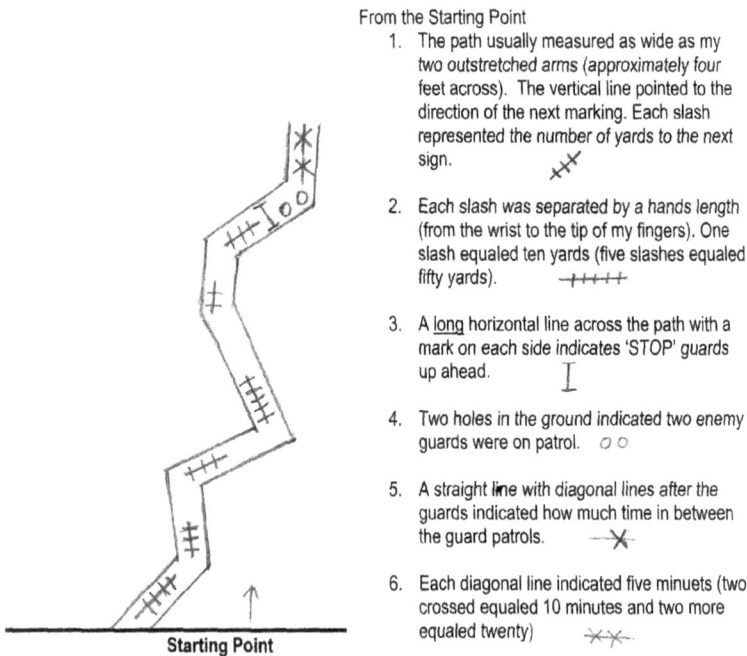

From the Starting Point

1. The path usually measured as wide as my two outstretched arms (approximately four feet across). The vertical line pointed to the direction of the next marking. Each slash represented the number of yards to the next sign.

2. Each slash was separated by a hands length (from the wrist to the tip of my fingers). One slash equaled ten yards (five slashes equaled fifty yards).

3. A <u>long</u> horizontal line across the path with a mark on each side indicates 'STOP' guards up ahead.

4. Two holes in the ground indicated two enemy guards were on patrol.

5. A straight line with diagonal lines after the guards indicated how much time in between the guard patrols.

6. Each diagonal line indicated five minuets (two crossed equaled 10 minutes and two more equaled twenty)

Starting Point

Figure 5 - Landmine Path Markings

94

"When I was done showing them, the Lieutenant handed me a map indicating where he speculated the Russian trucks might be. I glanced at the map and figured my destination was about three miles from us.

"I took all my ammo and all of theirs too. I figured they wouldn't need it since they were headed back. I crawled quickly and quietly in search of the two Russian patrols. Along the way, I hid bundles of ammo in different places. The purpose was twofold. Carrying ammo all the way was too heavy and, I also wanted ammo for later use. I imagined everywhere the enemy could possibly follow if they were chasing me back, and hid it in those places too.

"Time was elusive, it seemed like days, but it was only hours. I had to travel slow through mine fields and escape the detection of lookout towers. Finally, I arrived at the location, I was on top of a small hill and the trucks were below me. I crawled on my stomach and quietly positioned my rifle. The Lieutenant was right. There were two trucks.

"Snow was beginning to fall and I noticed a few of the soldiers were in white camouflage snow gear. I, too, had my snow gear. It looked like they had just arrived. I counted twelve soldiers in the back of each truck in addition to two more in the front: a driver and an officer. In all, there were twenty-eight. The men were being ordered into formation, they were falling in shoulder to shoulder, at arm's length and three deep.

"I thought to myself, 'This is too good to be true! Just the kind of target I was hoping for!' Quickly, I loaded the new APB bullets, took aim and bam! I shot and killed three at one time."

Ray broke in, "I bet you they were surprised,"

"They sure were," I said, "I'm sure they thought there was more than one enemy soldier shooting at them, but it was only me." I smiled and Ray started laughing.

"What happened after that?"

"Before they knew what was going on, I pin pointed three to four more soldiers clustered together, Bam, Bam, I fired again. When I fired these next two rounds, they all scattered. In the next few minutes I scanned the scene, trying to figure out who might be the officers, but I couldn't make out the markings on the uniforms, so the next best thing was to look for who was giving orders.

"My ability to think fast at any moment always helped me get out of tough situations, in this case, to save my life. I strategized, 'If I can identify their officers and shoot them in the head, it will create even more chaos among the soldiers.' I identified those targets and fired! It worked! Every shot was meant to kill. *"Kill them all or don't bother coming back,"* these were my orders. I knew that if I didn't kill the enemy first, then they would kill me."

"How long did the battle last?"

"All evening and into the night, and it became more difficult to see when snow started falling. It really got cold. At one point there was an exchange of intense fire and I think they thought they killed me. I lay real quiet. They couldn't see me because I had dug a hole in the snow and hid inside it. I was on my stomach, real still, clutching my M-I. Some of the soldiers were hiding in an open field and when they didn't see any movement, they stood up slowly and immediately began shooting in my direction. I could hear their bullets whizzing past my ears. All I wanted was to make my body sink deeper into the snow and become invisible."

"Were you scared?"

96

"I sure was! I was pressing my body so hard into the snow that I even wanted to remove the buttons on my field jacket so I could sink even deeper into the ground. I was praying their bullets wouldn't hit the ammo clips or one of the twenty hand grenades I had clipped to my cartridge belt. I felt frozen in that shallow hole. I saw my whole life pass before my eyes. I thought of my mom, my dad, my brothers, sisters, friends, and every place I had ever been to in the past. It seemed like hours, but it was only about twenty minutes. 'Catching quarters won't help me now!' I thought."

"How did you get out of there?"

"I regained my composure and began returning fire! It was kill or be killed. Once I snapped out of it, I had no sense of time nor did I worry about time. My only worry was to stay alive, killing them all, and to get the hell out of there before reinforcements arrived. We exchanged fire all night and by ten o'clock the next morning, I was the only soldier left standing. All the training, the mean Sergeants, the rough upbringing, what my brothers had taught me, everything kicked in, and I survived."

"You mean there wasn't anyone left but you?" Ray asked in disbelief.

"Not one! That was my job!"

Ray again asked, "They were all dead?"

"Yes, they were all dead. I made sure of it. When they told me to go back and make sure they were all dead, I did just that. As I walked up to the bodies, I didn't know what to expect. I forced myself to go up to each and every one of them, it was *'kill or be killed,'* I made sure none were left alive."

I took a deep breath and let it out slowly. As I exhaled, Ray heard me mutter... "That's been with me for a long, long time."

Ray was still trying to grasp the fact that I, his dad, had actually killed all those soldiers, and all by myself. I was only nineteen.

"What age did the other soldiers look like?"

"Same as us, eighteen, nineteen, twenty-four, twenty-five, there were two men that could have been thirty-five or forty, but those were probably officers."

"What did you do after that?"

"When I finally made it back to camp, only the officers remained, the rest of the squad had already left. It was nightfall when I walked into the front door of the Colonel's makeshift headquarters. Everyone there seemed surprised to see me. I walked in slowly, still trying to digest what had just happened. I was exhausted.

"Right away I heard, 'You lucky shit! We didn't expect you back, in fact, we didn't want you back!' And then there was laughter. I couldn't believe it!

"Instead of being treated with respect, I was being treated like an outsider who was disposable. The Lieutenant, Captain and one of the Sergeants were all in on it. I thought, 'Why are they being like this.' I had just saved their mission and instead of telling me, 'Hey, you did a good job!' They disrespected me like this!"

"Didn't that make you mad?"

"You better believe it." I could see it bothered Ray too. "That's one reason why I don't trust the government anymore. They take you real young, train you to do all their dirty work, use you, and then throw you out like you didn't even exist! The only one who didn't say anything the whole time was a Warrant Officer. It was bizarre, they treated me like dirt!"

"Why do you think they treated you like that?"

"Believe me; I thought about it a lot. Maybe they wanted to play with my mind so I wouldn't want any recognition for what I had just done. After all, I had just killed twenty-eight soldiers all by myself. I could take them out too… if I wanted. Maybe that was their strategy for keeping control over me. Either way, I was angry about the whole thing."

"'Why don't you just shut up?' I told them and walked off. I wanted one of them to throw me a punch so I could beat the hell out of him, or worse. They came 'This' close to dying," I motioned to Ray with my fingers.

"I turned my back to them and started to walk out. Just then I glanced over to a far corner in the room, the Colonel was sitting there. I hadn't noticed him before because those three idiots had my full attention. The Colonel was behind a desk with his arms propped behind his head and leaning back on his chair. His eyes made contact with mine. Without a spoken word, he gave me a thumbs-up "OK" sign with his hand.

"Five minutes later everyone was in the trucks, and we were headed back to Nuremberg.

"One of the Lieutenants sitting in the front seat turned his head around and said to me, 'You can't tell anyone where you've been, and you didn't hear anyone's name either! Understand?'

"I remained silent but deep inside I was very angry and about to explode. As soon as I got back to Ansbach, I got sick. The first two nights back in the barracks were miserable. I couldn't hold any food down. I was throwing up every little while and several times, I barely made it to the latrine to throw up. I felt as if my body was real hot.

"Life changed drastically for me after this mission. I felt I went from a nineteen year old to an old man. I constantly had this awful feeling in the pit of my stomach. I couldn't believe I had just killed all those men, and it seemed like nobody cared. It was as if I lost something, like I... ."

Ray was trying to help me find words for what I wanted to express, he asked, "Was it like losing your innocence?"

I tried hard to pin point the feeling, "No, it was worse… It was like I lost respect for life itself. I didn't care anymore. Time didn't seem to matter. Nothing mattered anymore. After that, I started to age, not on the outside, but inside. Life wasn't fun anymore. After that mission, I looked at everyone differently. I had no respect for anyone giving me an order.

"If someone even looked at me wrong, or if they came to give me orders, or even attempted to push me around, my thoughts were, 'Man, don't you mess with me! I'll go tonight to your bed! And if you think I don't know where you sleep?' I mean, I didn't care! I don't know how to explain what happened to me inside, I'm still having trouble with it. I honestly feel we're not supposed to kill......we're not supposed to kill!"

Ray sat there in silence. I saw he was without words. I knew he still wanted to ask me something and so he waited a while then he asked, "Dad, during that mission, did you make friends with anybody?"

"There was no time! All they had me doing was clearing the god damn mines then waiting all by myself like an idiot, and then sending me back to shoot all them Russians.

"In spite of the way I was feeling, the missions continued. One week later, I was leading another squad into enemy territory."

8

FIFTH MISSION

"The Code"

"I was waiting for our squad at our rendezvous point, suddenly I spotted one of our Sergeants come running up the path toward me. Twenty yards behind him, running like heck, was a young Lieutenant carrying a briefcase. It was very late in the afternoon and we were running out of daylight. In his haste, the Lieutenant wasn't paying attention where he was running and instead of taking a right turn like the markings indicated on the path, he ran straight. When he realized what he had done, he began shaking with fear realizing he had walked into an un-cleared minefield.

"We lost sight of him for an instant and the Sergeant freaked. 'The briefcase, I need the briefcase!' He frantically kept repeating.' I figured whatever was in it, must be very important.

"Next he ran up to me and got right in my face, "Go find that F...... briefcase and bring it back. It's more important than bringing that F...... Lieutenant back! Understand?"

"I looked at the Sergeant defiantly but didn't want to waste my time confronting him just then, so I left quickly to rescue the Lieutenant. I found him wandering around the mine field. I thought he was going to get himself blown up and by the frantic look on his face. He did too. In fact, he was so scared that he had shit in his pants.

"In a split second, every possible scenario flashed before my eyes. I knew that if I left him there, he would probably step on a landmine and get blown up. And if he didn't, eventually he would wander into the clearing and get shot by the guards in the lookout tower. Then the guard tower would surely spot the rest of the squad and kill them too.

"We still had people on the other side trying to make their way back, so either way, the enemy would spot us. I couldn't carry the Lieutenant and the briefcase at the same time so I left the briefcase and quickly snatched him and threw him over my shoulder. Shit from his pants smeared all over me, he stunk badly.

"I didn't care that I was told to bring the briefcase first; to me, saving this man's life was more important. I was all of 5'8', but I carried the soiled lieutenant like a sack of potatoes over my shoulder. I ran back to where the Sergeant was, dropped the Lieutenant on the ground, and returned for the briefcase.

"By the time I returned with the briefcase, another Lieutenant had arrived and was anxiously pacing back and forth waiting for me.

"'Sergeant!' he quietly yelled. I approached closer to hear what he had to say. 'We've been spotted… they're coming!' I saw the nervousness in his eyes.

"'How many' I asked.

"'Two trucks, you need to leave right now! Find them, and when you find them, stop them! Kill 'em all! Make sure they're all dead! Remember… LEAVE NO WITNESSES.' The Lieutenant gave me a piercing stare then said, *'If you can't kill them all, don't bother coming back!'*"

"Wasn't that what you were told in the last mission?" Ray asked.

"Sure was. At the time I thought, 'Hmm sounds familiar.' Anyway, I gathered all the ammunition I could carry and headed out.

"It was dark by the time I spotted the rest of our squad. I stopped for just a few minutes to make sure they remembered how to read my trail markings and continued on. I slipped through guard patrols and navigated through the foreign countryside at night looking for the enemy.

"It wasn't until early the next morning that I finally located the Russian trucks. I circled around and made my way to the top of a hill behind them. The soldiers had gotten off the trucks and I speculated they were preparing to look for us.

"I surprised them with gunfire before they were able to run for cover. With precision, I aimed at two and three at a time and hit my targets. We exchanged fire all day and into the night. I darted back and forth from tree to tree, shooting down at them. Eventually, they started closing in on me. I had to find an escape route.

"'Oh no,' I thought, 'The only way out is to slide down this hill.' And so I did, I slid down the hill on my back, clutching the rifle tightly to my chest. The ground was frozen hard and covered with a layer of snow. I slid down fast, swerving from side to side to avoid a deadly collision with oncoming trees.

"Suddenly, I felt myself slide into a well worn animal trail. I knew that when the Russians reached the top of the hill, I would be in clear view of them and they would come after me with a vengeance. I looked up and sure enough, I saw the flicker of their flashlights searching for me.

"'Alright!' I thought. 'Easy targets!' In a matter of seconds, I steadied the rifle above my head and aimed at the lights. Even though I was sliding down on my back and swerving from side to side, I hit my targets. They couldn't see me but I could sure see them. I reached the bottom of the hill with a thump and tumbled over on my stomach. I lay there still, only the sound of bullets whizzing close to my ears broke the silence."

All this time Ray was listening, engrossed in the story's details. I know he didn't want to interrupt me just yet.

"All of a sudden he started laughing, "You were like a bunny rabbit getting shot at by a rifle, weren't you!"

"Oh yeah, but I was too fast and too smart for them."

"How many were shooting at you at that point?" he asked.

"Do you mean when I got to the bottom of the hill?"

"Yeah"

"There were maybe eight, or nine."

"How many were there originally?"

"As many as the fourth mission, about twenty-eight."

Ray looked surprised, "You mean you had already shot that many? You had killed sixteen of them?"

"Oh yeah," I nodded sadly, "I picked them off real fast at first. As soon as they started chasing me, I made them think I was headed back towards the border but instead I kept circling around behind them and picking them off. They thought they were hunting me, but actually, I was hunting them."

"Were you wearing your white snow gear?"

"I was, and so were they, but only an idiot could not see them. They were easy to spot running while trying to shoot at me and that was a mistake. Not me, when I moved in the snow, I moved slowly and constant, slowly and constant, then waited. I had great vision and knew that if I waited long enough, one of them would stick their head up to look for me, then lower it, and

104

eventually stick it up again. Sure enough, and when that happened, BAM! One by one, I picked most of them off."

"Wow, Dad, when you slid down the hill, how long did you stay there?"

"It seemed like forever that I was lying there on my stomach. Finally, I rolled over onto my back and took the cover off my rifle's scope and began scanning the horizon. I shot a few more and then made the rest of them chase me into a mine field. By the time they realized what I was doing, it was too late, only seven survived.

"I shot and wounded one of the soldiers on purpose, hoping the other six would stay behind and help their wounded comrade, but they didn't, so I stopped firing. I wanted them to think I had run out of ammo, and to make it believable, I removed the clip from my rifle, stood up, and began shooting an empty barrel. They bought it, hook, line, and sinker. All six stood up even the wounded one, and began running towards me. As I ran for cover with my rifle, they didn't notice I had inserted a loaded clip.

"I heard a loud blast. One had stepped on a landmine. Now there were only five running after me. One soldier climbed up a tree to try and spot me. That, too, was a mistake; now there were only four left.

"I stopped momentarily and turned around. One of them was getting close. I could see the anger in his face as I waited for him to get closer, and then took him out too. The other three kept coming farther behind him. It was an officer and two soldiers, one of which was the one I had wounded on purpose. I stood up and aimed at them.

"The officer knew I had them in my sights. When he saw me, he threw his rifle to the ground, turned to his men and ordered them to do the same. The one that wasn't wounded didn't want to throw down his rifle and side arm. He really wanted to kill me. I could hear them yelling at each other. Slowly, I walked behind a tree and squatted down. They stopped arguing but by then, they couldn't see me.

"The officer looked toward my direction. He knew that wherever I was, I had a bead on them, and he was right. I stood up real slow so they could see me, and when the officer saw me, he stood at attention. He turned to the others so they could do the same. The officer saluted me, and I saluted him back. I let them turn around and slowly walk away as I looked on. I let them live."

"Had the young soldier picked up his rifle, would you have killed all of them?"

"Yes. I would've killed all three. When I let them go, I thought, 'I broke the CODE.'"

"What code?" Ray asked.

"THE CODE.... 'DON'T LEAVE ANYONE ALIVE!'"

"What did you do after that?"

"I stood watching until they disappeared into the trees."

"Were the other guys waiting for you when you got back?"

"Just two of them, it had been about a week since I had left base camp with the squad. Everyone else had already left except for the supply NCO, the guy in charge of issuing and keeping track of everything, and the one we called the "Cook." He wasn't really a cook; he just gave us our rations.

"These two guys stayed behind to make sure everyone got a ride back to Nuremburg. When I got there, I could tell the NCO was anxious to leave, he had the jeep all packed up. The "Cook" knew me pretty well and had faith I would make it back. He made sure the supply NCO didn't leave until I returned."

"What did you do when you returned to the base camp?"

"I headed straight for the bunker shower and then changed my clothes; they still smelled of shit from carrying that Lieutenant over my shoulder. As soon as I was done, we all hopped into the jeep and headed back to Nuremburg. I sat in the back quietly.

"'You know what?' the NCO said, 'You've lasted the longest clearing those landmines. The last guy you replaced blew himself up after the first mission. And the guys before that, backed out after their third mission.'"

"Did you feel pretty lucky? Ray asked.

"Yes, I had already survived five missions. I was just very glad my old instructor didn't give up on me even when I first couldn't see the landmines.

"We reached Nuremburg and there was already another jeep waiting to take me back to base. They left me off in Ansbach and I went directly to the barracks. Some of the guys from my platoon saw me arrive and came over to my bunk.

"'Where were you Frank? You've been gone a whole week. Everyone has been asking for you.' I didn't ask who 'they' were. I ignored their questions and went about my business. I couldn't tell them where I had been. Naturally, they assumed I was off doing something fun again.

"That night, I replayed every detail of the mission. For the first time, I had gone against orders. I broke the 'CODE.' Even so, I felt better inside and didn't throw up as much like before."

9

SIXTH MISSION

"Kill or Be Killed"

"I had no time to settle into a routine before I was off to another mission. This mission was different, there seemed to be more commotion than usual.

"I overheard two officers talking about bringing someone back alive. 'This time you're going with us, Sergeant.'"

"Why do you think they wanted you to go?" Ray asked, "You hadn't before."

"I'm not sure, but this was the first time I was instructed to stay with them for the entire mission. The guys on this mission were real fit. They were well trained soldiers. Two of them were assigned to help carry my supplies while I cleared landmines. These guys were all dressed in black and by their actions; I could tell they were good at whatever their assignment was.

"I cleared a path deep into enemy territory. We finally reached our destination. Far up ahead, I could see a small village. It appeared as if the village had been converted into a military base. I noticed Russian guards were patrolling the surrounding area. It was too dangerous for us to get nearer so we waited about a mile from the village until nightfall.

"Finally, we were given orders to approach the makeshift base with caution and take out the guards. I began creeping along the perimeter of the town, navigating in the dark shadows of the trees, careful not to be seen or heard.

"All of a sudden I came upon a Russian soldier a few feet ahead of me. Quietly, I snuck up right behind him and clamped my left hand tight over his mouth. I had a knife in my right hand and in one swift move cut his throat. Then, in another swift move, I slid the blade slowly into his side, half way into his ribs.

"I don't know what I was thinking, but I turned him around to see the expression on his face. I had anticipated looking him in the eye with an acknowledgment of victory; but instead the expression I witnessed, I was not ready for.

"There was a security light on the corner of one of the buildings in the village and the far off light barely shone on us. As I turned him around, I stared directly into his eyes, they were wide with shock and he was staring right at me as if asking, 'What happened?'

"He didn't know what hit him. I was stunned by the look in his eyes as he died in my arms. I pushed him off me quickly and guided him to the ground. The smell of human blood made me sick. I hunted as a boy and had killed animals and seen really bad cuts and wounds, but it was a whole lot different killing a human being up close. I could smell the warm blood seeping out from his wounds. It was steaming from the chilly night.

"That picture is forever imprinted in my memory. To this day, I still have flashbacks of that encounter. That was the first and last time I looked into the face of my enemy. After that, I made sure they were just targets.

"I don't know how many Russian soldiers we killed that night, but I do know that I was responsible for killing many of them. It was 'kill or be killed,' I convinced myself they were merely targets. I didn't dare look at their faces again.

"When I eliminated the guards, one of the Lieutenants motioned for me to remain at a distance. The soldiers in black were instructed to locate the enemy's command post and take it. In a matter of minutes, they brought out a top ranking officer in uniform and what appeared to me a scientist who was dressed in street clothes. Both were escorted to the center of the village.

"The scientist had an expression of surprise and fear. Within seconds, a couple of our guys had the scientist on the ground. They took off his shoes and fitted him with some special boots. They then wrapped a thick pad around his ankles and tied his feet together with a small cable.

"I looked on with intrigue as they wrapped him all up in something that resembled a straight jacket made of leather. They slipped a mask with two eye openings over his head and over this, a cloth sack. Then in another swift move, they wrapped tape around his neck and continued all the way down the rest of his body. The guy looked like a mummy. Everything was done real fast. They definitely knew what they were doing."

"Do you think he was expecting it?" Ray asked.

"No way, I think he probably thought we were going to kill him."

"What happened next?"

"They got two long cables which were maybe six hundred feet long and clipped one end to each of his boots. At the other end of each cable were what looked like three real big weather balloons? I'm guessing they were filled with helium gas.

"I heard, 'GO!' And instantly the balloons swooped up and lifted the scientist off the ground. They did the same thing to the other guy, the officer, and seconds later he was gone too."

"Gone where?" Ray asked.

"Gone! Man, they were gone! I looked up in the sky and heard an airplane somewhere above the clouds. I could see the balloons but only for about one hundred feet and then they faded into the night and above cloud cover. When we left, no one was left alive, that is, as far as I knew.

"On our way back I overheard the guys in black talking to each other, 'He's one of the best we've seen.' They were talking about me. I didn't know what to think of that.

"'Hey Sergeant,' one of them said, 'How about joining our unit.' I overheard them talking about asking their superior to draft me into their unit.

"'Hell no'... I said right away. 'I don't want to come over here with you guys. No Way! I wanna go back to 'MY' base.'

"We drove to Nuremburg and stopped at a pub and drank beer. This was a first. After a few hours I left. The other guys stayed and I hopped on a jeep that was headed back to Ansbach."

10

THE SEVENTH AND FINAL MISSION

"That's Where It Ended"

"Wasn't this your final mission... the seventh?" Ray asked. He knew it would be hard for me to talk about it and I already knew that once I started talking about it, I wouldn't be able to sleep tonight. "Are you sure you're up for it today, Dad?" Ray asked again.

"I'm as ready as I can be" and so I began.

"It was 1959, I can't remember the exact date, but it was toward the end of September." I looked at Ray, "I still have a hard time remembering details. It was a long time before I could even talk about it."

"How did it start?" Ray asked.

"I was in Ansbach and we were all lining up in formation after lunch when a couple of officers from headquarters came to talk to the first Sergeant of my unit.

"They left and the First Sergeant continued to assign the day's duties and then he yelled out 'Trash Detail... Wiggins! Graseck! Pitman! Rodriguez!' He gave us our orders.

"The other three guys went in one direction and my orders instructed me to report to battalion headquarters. At battalion headquarters, I boarded a waiting jeep and we headed toward Nuremburg. In Nuremberg, we then drove to a base bigger than the one in Ansbach. As usual, my connection was waiting near the 'Post Office'."

"Was that like your rendezvous point?"

"Yes, there was always someone there waiting to take me to the "Guard House." This is where we always selected our supplies, changed clothes, and loaded up on ammo and food. Essentially, we loaded up on everything needed for a mission.

"We arrived at the guard house and there was a big truck, a canvas covered deuce and half, parked out front. There was also a jeep. Both vehicles had just arrived. A Colonel stepped down from the jeep and entered the guard house. The place was full of equipment and supplies. Other soldiers from different bases were there too and we all packed our stuff in silence. None of us ever had any form of identification except for our dog tags.

"The Colonel himself walked up and handed each of us our rank, a removable sleeve that went over our left arm. Mine was always a Buck Sergeant.

"He looked at me sort of proudly and said *'This is your seventh. You're the best we've ever had for landmines.'*

"How did he know who you were?" Ray asked.

"I don't know. He had been with us a few times and to my recollection this Colonel is the only one in all my missions to ever give me some form of recognition."

"Did you know anyone else there?"

"Just one officer, a Captain. In prior missions, I usually recognized two or three faces, but this time there were none except for the Captain and Colonel. The Captain had an attitude; he acted like he was a General or some other hot shit. From the minute I arrived that day, he singled me out."

"What did he do?" Ray asked.

"While I was packing my gear I felt the Captain's presence standing right behind me. I heard him say, 'Why are you taking

114

that?' He pointed to my beef jerky. 'And candy bars? He said, 'You ought to be taking something more nutritious.'

"I didn't pay him any attention. I just continued packing my supplies. I walked over to pack my ammo and took some boxes of APB's.

"'Take the other bullets!' He shouted, 'Those are too expensive!'

"He practically ran toward me and stuck his hand in my pack and took some of the APB's out. I merely opened up another box and packed those. The Captain became frustrated because I didn't let his attitude bother me.

"'You take what you want, and I'll take what I want.' I said to him as I continued packing. I got him so pissed off that when I stood up he got right in my face.

"'As soon as we get back I'm going to file a report on you!'

"I still pretended not to get bothered. I didn't care what he said. Those bullets were going to save my life and that's all that mattered to me."

"Why did he have it out for you?"

"I don't know; something about me bothered him. Maybe he didn't like the fact that I didn't react to his silly orders."

"What happened next?"

"I hustled and finished packing everything. The big deuce and half pulled up close and we were signaled to jump in. I noticed that behind the truck was the Colonel's jeep. Waiting in it was the driver and two soldiers. I never knew what was really up and so I was always vigilant of every detail. I glanced over at the two soldiers in the Colonel's jeep; underneath their uniforms, they had civilian clothes. Nothing was ever what it seemed.

"I jumped into the back of the canvas covered truck. To my surprise, the truck was full of people. The Captain was seated toward the front, right behind the cab, and when he saw me sit by the tailgate he immediately told me, 'You can't sit there, get out of there!'

"My piercing eyes glared at him. I was looking for a good excuse to kick his ass. He just wouldn't let up. I thought to myself, 'If you want to come back alive, better not mess with me.' I didn't move and that pissed him off more.

"I noticed that after every mission I changed and my attitude changed. By now, I really didn't care what they told me because every time I saved their lives, they treated me like crap afterwards. These were not ordinary situations. The Captain wasn't showing me any respect and I sure wasn't going to show him any either. He finally got it and left me alone.

"It was quiet in the truck. I looked around. There were six Germans and judging by their expressions, they were not happy campers. My first impression was that they were some sort of VIP's and got the feeling they weren't too happy where we were headed to. At least they probably knew our destination. I leaned my back against the truck canvas wall and counted the hours.

"The Colonel's jeep was following pretty far behind us. Sometimes it would approach our truck and then slow down until it was out of sight. Then within a half hour or so, it would catch up again. I always made it a point to sit close to a truck's tailgate because I liked to have a view of the road behind us. By my way of thinking, I had a fast exit in case of approaching danger. I was on survival mode, twenty-four seven.

"It was very quiet in the truck and, after a few hours the Germans tried to make small talk."

116

"What did they say?" Ray asked.

"They wanted to know which base each one of us was from."

"What did you say?"

"Nothing, I just looked at them and nodded my head. Our orders were not to engage in conversation so I nodded my head in agreement and let them think whatever they wanted.

"The two VIP's kept to themselves. I overheard them discussing something about the mission. I could understand a little German and knew that these two were responsible for bringing some sort of information back and we had to ensure their safety.

"We drove for quite a while and only stopped briefly to eat. The drivers pushed on late into the night until we finally arrived at our destination. The truck came to an abrupt stop and everyone grabbed their gear and jumped off.

"We all entered what seemed like an ordinary German house but on the inside it was one of our installations. When I entered, I looked around and saw several big conference rooms and three other rooms which appeared to be for lodging. I looked out the front door and just then the Colonel's jeep arrived and he stepped out. The Colonel immediately came inside and gathered his officers together to one of the conference rooms. He glanced behind him to the other room and motioned for the rest of the soldiers to enter the conference room too. He hesitated momentarily, then looked at me and a Corporal who standing next to me. The Colonel motioned with his hand for us to stay put."

"How come you and the Corporal were left out?"

"At first I thought nothing of it. I just figured they were going to discuss information we didn't need to know."

"Did you leave?"

"Not right away, I waited until he finished saying something to his officers.

"The Colonel looked around at everyone in the room and with a very serious voice said, 'we're going to be gone a little longer than usual, and this time, we have to go further in.' He looked at me, 'You! You don't need to go all the way with us. You can leave. Go to one of the rooms and bed down... you too, Corporal.'"

"Who was that Corporal?"

"At the time I didn't know the Corporal was there to assist me. I was about to leave when out of nowhere the Captain stood in front of me preventing me from leaving.

"For some reason he didn't want me to bed down just yet. I barely had started to say I needed rest to do my job when he rudely interrupted me, 'Stand at attention, Sergeant, and shut up!' The Captain turned to the Colonel and said, 'I think this soldier should stay and listen!'

"The room stirred with tension. Everyone could see the Colonel was annoyed with the Captain's insubordinate behavior. The Colonel looked sternly at the Captain, 'This soldier needs to clear the landmines! He needs to be alert!' He gave the Captain a cold stare, 'Do you want to come back in one piece?' The room was quiet. The Captain turned red and reluctantly acknowledged the Colonel's comments. 'Then sit down and listen!' The Colonel demanded of the Captain, 'This man needs to get some sleep!'"

Ray looked surprised, "How did you feel when the Colonel told the Captain off?"

"Good! I felt the Captain finally got what he deserved. I grinned with pleasure as I turned around to turn in for the night."

"Do you think the Captain saw you grin?"

118

"I don't know, but I sure hope he did.

"At six o'clock in the morning I was shaken out of my sleep by a Lieutenant, 'Wake up, it's time for you to go work and do your magic.'

"By the time I packed all my gear and went for breakfast, it was already seven o'clock. Everyone else was still asleep. As usual, they rested and slept during the day because, come nightfall, they had to travel and stay awake all night.

"When I finished breakfast I asked the Lieutenant, 'Do you want me to start right away?'

"'No,' he answered, 'They might see you!'"

'Well, the thing is,' I explained, 'It might take me two hours to have the one path cleared going over and if I start now, I can clear the second path coming back before it gets dark. I'll have the two paths done quickly.'

"The Lieutenant hesitated for a moment, 'Okay, go for it,' he answered."

"Did that Corporal go with you?' Ray asked.

"No, he was supposed to though, but I didn't know that until later. I don't think the Lieutenant knew it either because he was the one who was supposed to wake up the young Corporal. As a matter of fact, the Cook didn't know it either or he would have prepared two sack lunches. If I had seen two sack lunches, I definitely would have asked who the other one was for.

"I headed out by foot and hiked two to three miles by the time I reached the mind fields. I had done this so many times that the routine was already boring. Even so, I kept my eyes open and didn't engage in aimless thinking. Any clumsy action on my part and the Russian guard towers might spot me.

"It took two hours to clear the first path from landmines. My mind was busy, my hands were busy, and two hours felt like fifteen minutes. Since I was doing good time, I went further into enemy territory just to make sure there weren't more short mine fields. I had already encountered several."

"What are short mine fields?"

"Sometimes the Russians would plant land mines up to a certain point, stop for a short distance, then continue to plant more. They did this to trick their enemy into thinking there were no mines beyond a certain area."

"You did something similar with the 'V' didn't you?"

"Similar, but mine was a booby trap designed to kill a whole squad. About a quarter mile up ahead, I spotted a small rugged arroyo. 'Yeah,' I thought, 'This is a good landmark.' and I begun to clear a path all along its border.

"I thought, 'If the squad gets spotted on their return and they're in a hurry to get back, I'll tell them to follow the arroyo.' I was always thinking about all possible scenarios and how to secure the safety of the squad. I ran quietly without being detected along the ditch and shrubs just to make sure I hadn't missed any land mines. The entire process took me about four hours and still, I had time left so I planted about fifty small and big booby traps in other locations. It was dusk when I finally finished and knew that by this time, the squad had already started coming down the path toward me. I found a good hiding place and waited for them.

"For some reason, they took longer than usual and didn't reach me until dawn the following morning.

"'Did you clear both places?' asked a Lieutenant.

"'Yes, I cleared two paths. When we cross I'll show you where they are and how I marked them. One of them is along an arroyo.' I was glad I didn't need to talk to the smart ass Captain. He and a couple of the other officers were looking at a map. I was surprised to see the Colonel came along for this mission.

"We slept under trees and brush during the day and as soon as it got dark, they prepared to leave. To my understanding, I was going with them just up to a certain point, then stay behind until their return, and who knows how long that would be."

"Did you know where they were going?" asked Ray.

"They mentioned a town but I can't remember its name. A few of the guys on this mission were big. They looked strong and healthy. The officers handed them their heavy packs to carry. Another big soldier grabbed the Colonel's pack and the officer's rifles. Can you believe it?" I told Ray, "They also brought a soldier to help me! It was the Corporal who I had left sleeping."

"Did you need help?" Ray asked.

"At the time I didn't think so, but afterwards, I was glad he was there.

"When I first found out he was there for me, I asked a Lieutenant, 'Why did you bring him?'

"'He's going to help you carry your ammo and he's also trained like you, to clear landmines.'

"Suddenly I recalled what the supply NCO had said to me the last mission. 'You know what? You've lasted the longest clearing landmines. The last guy you replaced blew himself up after the first mission and the guys before that backed out after the third mission.' I guess they figured my days were numbered. This young corporal was my backup; in other words, my replacement. They didn't want the mission jeopardized if I got blown up!

"That night we covered a lot of distance. I stopped to take another look at the map they had given me. It indicated that somewhere up ahead there were some factories or some kind of big buildings. We slowed the pace down. I think they were getting tired carrying the heavy packs. Every once in a while the big guys would exchange packs with each other. I wondered what they had in those packs, and where they were going with all this stuff.

"Finally we reached the squad's departure point and the Corporal was instructed to stay behind with me. That was a surprise! After they left, we had a lot of time on our hands. I wasn't used to having someone wait with me and this Corporal asked a lot of questions. Even so, I liked the guy. He didn't seem to be full of bullshit.

"I wanted to keep busy so I set out to create a new return path. All the while, he kept his eyes on me, observing everything I was doing and seemed fascinated that I was so thorough. He was amazed that I had cleared two mine fields in one day. I wasn't doing it to impress, I did what I did to stay alive!

"As we talked I could tell the Corporal was still disappointed that no one had awakened him before I left the camp the day before. He told me he was looking forward to learn some new techniques.

"We sat down for a little while and talked. 'You know, usually guys that do what you do only last so long. Most get killed, and if they don't get killed, they get their arms or legs blown off.' Obviously, the young Corporal didn't realize yet, the same thing might happen to him.

"It seemed like forever before the squad returned. That forever time I paid for dearly for not bringing more food. Like always, I had brought more ammo and only a few candy bars and some beef jerky. Luckily, the Corporal had brought plenty of food and he kept me fed. He actually kept me from starving.

"I was eating some of his rations and said, 'You know, normally I don't bring food at all, I just bring ammo.'

"The Corporal responded, 'I wasn't too worried about bringing that much ammo. I was told they hardly ever encountered any Russian soldiers on these missions.'

"Hearing that pissed me off, 'Well, they lied to you! My first two missions were more or less a practice run. This is my seventh and the ones in between... well those missions were combat to the max. That's for sure!'

"He looked at me with wide eyes as I told him how it really was. I continued, 'During all the missions I always stayed behind and when they returned, they sent me to fight and kill the enemy who had spotted them. Like a fool, I believed they would follow and help me, but they never did. I don't trust any of those guys at all! I don't believe anything they say, and half of what I see I don't believe is true.' The Corporal looked at me in disbelief."

"Was the Corporal that naïve?" Ray asked.

"No, he just hadn't been around them as long as I had."

"The Corporal was soon to find out this mission was no different. The squad got back four days later around midnight. They came scurrying through the trees and shrubs.

"The Colonel was one of the first to arrive, 'Take the Corporal with you to help you take some charges! Quick…. we need a building blown up right away!' One of others who had just arrived drew me a little map on a piece of paper and pointed to the building they wanted blown up.

"I asked, 'Should I check it out first to see if there's anyone in it?'

123

"'I didn't give you those orders!' The Colonel shot back quickly, 'I told you I wanted the building down! I don't care about anything else!'

"While they were showing me the map, the Corporal had already loaded two packs with charges. It was slow moving making our way at night, but we made good time. It had been snowing on and off during the last few days. Fortunate for us, the white snow reflected just enough light and that helped us travel faster. We reached the building about three o'clock in the morning.

"We both crept closer to the building, there was some kind of military sign staked out in front, but I couldn't read Russian, or whatever language it was written in. The Corporal couldn't read it either. I felt like the blind leading the blind, both of us couldn't read the signs.

"I knew there was a possibility that enemy soldiers might come running out of the building at any time and in that case, I would have to kill. In the back of my mind, I could hear the orders from prior missions, "kill them all, or don't bother coming back'.

"I darted ahead and began setting up the charges around the building. There was this one window in back of the building and all the while, I had the urge to go look in. I hesitated to look in the window, the Colonel's orders ran through my mind, 'I told you I want the building down! I don't care about anything else!'

"It was really dark but I thought I saw a slight movement at that window. I so badly wanted to look inside but again the Colonel's orders rang in my ears.

"As I was setting the charge I kept thinking, "What if I go to the window, maybe there's a little candle or some kind of light inside, maybe I can see if there's something or someone in there.' But then I didn't go, even though I wanted to so badly.

"I set up the second charge and again thought I saw something resembling a face come to the window. The Corporal and I were in the shadows and knew we couldn't be seen. I wanted to go up to that window and look inside but I didn't.

"I secured both charges to the wall of the building and sent the Corporal off to wait for me. I also put two big land mines with the charges and then attached a detonation cord to each charge. Each fuse was timed to go off in fifteen minutes. I lit both and immediately sprinted off. I could run! Both of us did double time. We both wanted to get away from there as soon as possible.

"Fifteen minutes later, the Corporal and I heard one big blast. We waited for the second one to go off, but it never came.

"'We need to go back and see what happened to the other charge!' said the Corporal panting. We had run so hard he was now doubled over trying to catch his breath.

"'I'll go, stay here,' I told him. I took off running like a mad man. I knew that if anyone was in the building and survived, they would be coming out pretty soon. The whole right side of the building was nearly gone. Only a big charge could do that.

"'I knew it!' I said to myself. 'The charges went off simultaneously, that's why we only heard one big blast.' I didn't see any movement outside so I started entering the building from the side that was still partially intact.

"I walked slowly into the dark building. After a few steps, I felt something stuck on my boot. I shook my foot but couldn't take it off. We wore those Mickey Mouse boots made of rubber so I couldn't tell what was stuck on it.

"I searched deep into my pocket and took out a flashlight. I removed the front cover off and inserted a little red glass with a cross shaped opening about an inch and half. The lens was designed to shine a minimal amount of light. I pointed the light at the floor and searched for what was stuck on my boot. I shook my foot then kicked my heel. It felt like part of a ball was stuck to it. I bent down and pulled it off and pointed the light on it... Dear God! It was a little skull! I was stunned! My eyes were fixated on the empty cavity.

"As far as I could tell it was the skull of a little human being, a kid. A little kid that was dead. The back of the skull was blown off and all I could see was the back of the eye sockets. I wanted to piss, shit, and throw up all at the same time! I was sick.

"Immediately, I began looking on the floor for the rest of the body, to see if there were little arms, little legs or little bodies. All the furnishings in the room were mangled like a tornado had hit the place. I searched frantically. That's all I could do so I wouldn't start crying. As tears began to fill my eyes, I thought, 'Look what we killed! What **I** killed! I should have listened to my intuition! I should have looked into the window like I wanted to!'

"As quietly as I could, I walked to the middle of the room. I saw a little arm and little leg with chains clasped around the wrist and ankle. They weren't attached to anyone or anything. I was sickened! I could only imagine what had been going on with these little children.

"I could see stairs off in a corner; they were leading up to another room on a second floor that had survived the explosion. I was so shocked by what I was seeing that the sounds coming from the room upstairs were drowned out. It felt like an eternity, but only a few minutes had gone by.

"I heard noise coming from a corner of the room and slowly I walked over. There, lying against a wall, I found a little girl, that is, what remained of a little girl. She had probably been blown there by the impact of the blast. I really wasn't sure if it was a little girl or boy because it had no legs from the waist down. Oh my God.....The child had nothing down there! All I could see was the cavity where the intestines were ready to fall out. It was horrifying!

"In the darkness I knelt down and lifted the child in my arms and gently sat with what was left of her in the corner. I couldn't believe this mangled little creature still had some life! I'm still not sure in which language she spoke to me, but she did. German or English, I understood what she said.

"In a faint voice she whispered, 'Soldiers…. There are soldiers on the next floor up.' Her eyes faintly looked at the stairs. She could barely talk but was determined to tell me. 'Follow those steps, they're all up there.' Tears were streaming down my eyes as she motioned with a nod of her head for me to get closer.

"I put my ear close to her lips, 'knock three times…. Like this… Ta ….Ta-Ta. They….. Torturing us ... You! ...... Go upstairs ….. Kill them for me….'

"And I did! I turned around with an anger I couldn't contain. Because of what I had just done, I wanted to take it out on somebody. If there was someone up there, they hadn't come running out yet, and I needed to get up there quickly. I knocked on the door as the little girl had said, and the door opened.

"A dim candle light illuminated the room. I saw some Russian soldiers trying to get their clothes on. The Russian who opened the door started walking away fast, not even looking in my direction when he opened the door. He probably thought it was one of the kids who had survived the blast. I was enraged, and as he walked away, I shot him. In a matter of seconds, I killed every one of them! I made sure of that!

"I ran back downstairs to the little girl to tell her it was all done! I crouched down. I don't know if I imagined it, but she had a faint smile and seemed to be looking straight at me. Her pupils were dark and gigantic. I knew she was gone.

"I was so angry! I walked outside overcome with anger and vengeance, and began walking down the road. I was walking straight up, not even hiding, and I didn't care if I was spotted by any guard towers. I was in search of my officers. I went looking for the Colonel and Lieutenant who gave me the orders! I wanted to shoot them for what they made me do. Tears were streaming down my face and I began running... running....running!

"I reached the mine field and ran right through it. I didn't even run through the areas I had cleared. I just ran. I took a short cut. I didn't even think about getting myself blown up. Finally, I located the trail back to the base camp, the makeshift headquarters.

"I reached the house and went inside looking for the officers. Everyone was gone, even the Corporal.

"Only a Sergeant and the 'Cook' were still there waiting for me.

"'They left. They thought you didn't make it,' said the Cook. 'They ordered us to leave but we wanted to wait. They really did think you were dead but we knew you would be back!'

"I couldn't calm the fury I felt and demanded to know the whereabouts of the Colonel and Lieutenant. 'I'm looking for that damn Colonel, I want to kill him!'

"The Sergeant responded, 'We were ambushed from the guard towers, the Colonel got shot, he's wounded real bad! The Lieutenant took charge, but he's wounded too!'

"'Where did they go?' I asked impatiently.

"'The Colonel is on his way to the hospital, but I don't think he's going to make it.'

"'I don't care,' I demanded. 'Take me to them!'

"'I don't know to which hospital they took him. All I know is that we have orders to go back.' The Sergeant was pacing and ready to leave. He motioned for us to get into the jeep quickly. I had no choice. I got in and we headed back to Nuremburg.

"When we arrived back at Nuremburg, the officers who were supposed to meet us were not there. We learned they were checking on the whereabouts of the Colonel and Lieutenant. I finally came to the realization that I couldn't do any more and so they drove me back to Ansbach.

"This had been one of the longest missions yet. We had been gone eighteen days. Right before I left on this mission, my friends had been planning a birthday party for me. I had left on the 25th of September and returned October the 12th. My birthday had been on October 10th. The minute I arrived back at the barracks, my friends wanted to celebrate. They had already paid for my birthday party and were ready to party.

"They tried to get me to go, but I couldn't. 'Go without me.' I didn't care anymore about anything. They had no idea what I had just been through. In my mind, October 10th never did arrive. I never celebrated my birthday. I never made it to twenty.

"I was nineteen when I left for that seventh mission and that's where I stayed stuck in my mind. I'm going to be seventy years old, and to this day, I still don't feel like I've reached twenty.

"Dr. Timothy Schuster, one of my therapists at the VA hospital, once told me that this experience traumatized me so severely that it triggered something in my brain which kept me younger because I could not go past that point. Coincidentally, he told me that he, too, was in Germany at the very same time that I was. He said it was common knowledge that missions such as the ones I was involved in, were going on.

"Two weeks had passed after that seventh mission and I had refused to do anything. They wanted me to go on more 'trash details' but I outright refused. They tried to get me to do menial stuff and I would snap back, 'Do it yourself!' I walked around with my carbine locked and loaded all the time.

"One day the MP's were dispatched to come and get me. They wanted to take my rifle away. I saw them coming and before they knew it, I had them both on the ground. I knew they were just doing their job, so before I wound up shooting my own people, I handed them my rifle.

"I was continually harassed. Officers I didn't even know came looking for me to take me on more missions. 'I told you I'm not going!'

"'You have to go!' they insisted.

"'No I don't! And you can't make me!'"

"That's incredible Dad, what did you do during that time?"

"I spent a lot of time drinking. I drank a lot and I also cried a lot. I stayed on my bunk all day and wouldn't go outside. I wasn't eating regularly and couldn't hold anything down. I started getting real depressed and even stopped hanging around with friends. I didn't care about anything. Life was nothing. I felt like an old man in a nineteen year-old body, but I actually was twenty. I didn't want to go anywhere; I couldn't even watch a movie. Nothing was fun and I hated everyone.

"There were several officers I didn't like and when they tried to order me around, I thought, 'Don't mess with me, man, I know where you sleep, I'll go at night and cut your throat!' I had a deep anger in my soul. They seemed to know what I was thinking.

"One afternoon an officer finally convinced me to leave the barracks. As I was lining up in formation that day, a carrier delivered a dispatch to one of the Sergeants. It was a message from the Red Cross, and it was for me. My mother had a heart attack and they wanted me to come home before it was too late. I was ordered to report to command headquarters immediately."

"Did you leave to California right away?" Ray asked.

"No, they didn't want to give me time to come home."

"Why?" I could see Ray was bothered. "When your mother is dying they're supposed to let you go home."

"But they didn't," I told Ray. "They said I could go only if I agreed to put in more time."

"You mean only if you re-enlisted?"

"Yes," I remember that day very clearly. The Sergeant's name was Maybee. He told me, 'Wiggins I need you to train somebody to do the job you were doing, that's the only way you can quit!'

"I told him 'Nope! I already told you I'm not going out there anymore! I don't know what part of it you don't understand!'"

"So they didn't let you go home?" Ray asked again.

"No! My mother didn't die but the stroke left her partially paralyzed."

"Couldn't you appeal?"

"To whom? They didn't care about anything but their missions."

"They continued to make life rough for me. They dispatched soldiers to pick me up and go clean this and that or to

131

pick up trash. Basically, they wanted me to do a bunch of dumb stuff which they could have easily gotten someone else to do. They were persistent in pressuring me to go out again. They came around one more time to get me to go on a mission.

"'Wiggins, you have to go with us!'

"I answered with a lethal stare, 'If I do….. NONE of you are making it back!'

"They ran out of patience and shortly after that day, I was handed my discharge papers.

"'Wiggins! You're going home!'"

11

HONORABLY DISCHARGED

"Abandoned"

"After leaving Germany, I arrived at Fort Dixon, New Jersey and about two weeks later, I was officially discharged. It was January of 1960. I served one year, eleven months, thirteen days and ten hours. I didn't complete my entire tour, but they still gave me an honorable discharge. They left me there in New Jersey. I had only one month's pay in my pocket and was told to go home."

"Weren't you supposed to be discharged from your original recruitment station?" Ray asked.

"Yes, I was supposed to be discharged to Fort Ord or to Oakland, California."

"Why didn't they return you there?"

"They were still playing games and trying to make it rough on me. Somebody had to issue those orders. I was in such bad shape, mentally, that they probably thought I wouldn't make it back home, and they were almost right.

"When I arrived in the States I still had the rank of Sergeant, but as soon as I got to Fort Dix, my rank was knocked down to a private. At that time, the pay for a private was ninety-two dollars a month. The Army paid me ninety-two dollars and deducted ten dollars which they claimed was for shoes I hadn't turned in.

"I went to the airport to buy a ticket home, but it cost two-hundred and seventy-two dollars. Obviously, I didn't have enough money. All I had was eighty-two dollars. I didn't have any place to go so the only thing I could think of was to go back to the Base. I left the airport and found my way to the subway station and headed back to Fort Dix, New Jersey."

"Weren't you already discharged?" Ray asked.

"Yes, but I didn't have any place to stay."

"What did you do?"

"Even though I was all messed up, instinctively, I knew how to survive. I arrived back at Fort Dix and hung around close to the base and blended in with the other soldiers. There were so many soldiers, the guards didn't know I was already discharged, and so I just walked back into the Base. I spent the first night in the guard shack and the next morning I got up early and went to breakfast at the battalion mess hall. That's where all the soldiers who were just reporting to Fort Dix ate. I knew they would have a hard time telling I didn't belong there.

From there, I walked over to where the new transfers check in. I looked around and picked up a duffel-bag full of uniforms intended for one of the new transfers. I made sure it was a bag designated for a first or second lieutenant. I needed money, so I went to one of the big subway stations where I sold the contents of the entire bag. I got two-hundred dollars for the clothes.

I went back to the Base and again walked right by the guards and again, I spent the night in the guard shack. Nobody asked any questions. After breakfast, I picked up another duffel-bag and this time caught the subway to New York. I found out I could get more money there for the bag's contents. With the money I got, I rented a room in New York and got drunk.

"During the next three weeks I went back to the Base five

more times and did the very same thing."

"Wow, Dad," Ray said laughing, "You were crazy."

"I was sick! I didn't realize I had enough money in my pocket to buy me an airplane ticket back home. I was drinking heavily and didn't know I had PTSD. I just worried about making more money to get a room.

"During that month I met a lot of people who were really good to me. Some even invited me to lunch and didn't let me pay for anything. Others invited me to their house. They knew I had just come from Germany and wanted to hear stories. If they had kids, the kids would often take a liking to me. Some kids would even ask their parents if I could spend the night. I think the kids could sense the hurt in my heart. I tell you, the people I met in New York were the best and the kindest I've ever met.

"They were curious about my experience while I was in Germany. I sure didn't want to tell them the truth. I only told them about Elvis Presley and how he had just left when I arrived. Elvis left a great impression for all Americans that went to Germany at that time. Elvis Presley was a great ambassador for the United States. When I told this to my friend Andy, he wasn't at all surprised to hear that about Elvis."

"So how did you finally get home, Dad?"

"One day I sobered up. I woke up in a motel room I had been renting and had a huge hangover. I wasn't thinking clearly. I sat up in bed and began shuffling through my wallet.

"All of a sudden I snapped, 'I have enough money to go home! What the heck am I doing here?' As soon as I made this realization, I packed up what little I had and headed for the airport.

"New York is a big city but luckily I ran into another soldier who helped me. I asked him, 'Hey man, can you help me get to the airport?'

"The soldier answered, 'I have to make a few phone calls first, but yes, I can get you there.' And he did. I tried to give him money but he wouldn't take it.

"I bought my ticket and still had money left. They almost didn't let me buy the ticket. I guess I still smelled of alcohol and most likely, I must have been still a little drunk.

"'Sir, if you're not completely sober by the time your flight is scheduled to leave, you will not be able to board the plane.'

"I had about an hour and a half to wait for the flight so I drank lots of coffee and when it was time to board, they let me get on. It had been at least a month since I was discharged when I finally arrived back home in LA. I still can't remember the exact date but it was in late February of 1960.

"I drank every day and every night after getting home. I couldn't sleep and the nightmares were especially bad if I went to bed early. My hearing was hyper sensitive and I could hear everything that went on in the neighborhood. I could hear all the dogs in the neighborhood barking as well as all the cats crying and fighting.

"At that time my parents lived in Wilmington. Their house was located near Main Street and Pacific Coast Highway. I could hear the noise of cars and trucks constantly passing. Harbor Freeway was about half a mile away and I could hear those cars on the freeway after midnight. The nights were very long."

"Had your family always lived in Wilmington?" Ray asked.

"Oh no, we lived in Torrance, Lomitas, Harbor City and San Pedro."

"Did you hang out with any friends?"

"No. More than a week had passed since I had arrived home. Finally my Dad told me I should go visit my brothers and sisters in San Jose. He was worried. Since I got home, he noticed I was drinking a lot and just moping around the house. I didn't want to do anything or see anyone. Basically I had become a loner."

"Which sisters were living in San Jose at that time?"

"Annabel and Mildred, my plans were to visit them for just a week. Instead, it turned out to be more like three weeks. First I visited Annabel and Mildred and then my friends Simon and George. My Dad had lent me his 1960 green Chevy and I had a good time visiting and driving around in his car."

"Dad, you said your mom had a heart attack when you were in Germany, was she alright when you got home?'

"Not quite. My mother was very happy that I was home. When I returned from San Jose, I spent a lot of time with her. We talked about a lot of things and yet nothing. The stroke had left her left arm and left part of her face paralyzed.

"I convinced her into letting me massage her arm and face. I hoped that eventually she might recover from her paralysis. Every day for three weeks, I massaged her.

"Then one day, about three o'clock in the morning, my mom woke me up yelling excitedly. 'Frankie! Frankie! ….wake-up! Look! I can move my arm and look at my face! … It's normal again!'

"Tears streamed down her face. 'Are you crying mom?'

"'Yes, but they're happy tears.' She didn't care what time it was, she called the whole family to tell them the good news."

12

LIVING ON THE EDGE

"A Walk in the Park"

"I got a job working with my Dad and our friend Abe, at an oil refinery. We were working in a huge ditch leveling the ground and laying concrete which was meant to hold oil pipes.

"One day, close to quitting time, everyone was talking about what they were going to do after work. I was so used to working out that I wanted to go exercise at a park.

"'I think I'm going for a walk in the park, I need to exercise.'

"'Which park?' Abe asked with a hint of concern in his voice.

"'The one between Wilmington and Long Beach, by the refineries.'"

"'No… don't go there, they might hurt you, they may even kill you! The cops don't even go there!' Abe looked at me real serious, 'The gangs run those parks. There's been murders and rapes! I tell you, it's real bad! Don't go there!' That didn't scare me. I decided to go anyway.

"Unknown to me at the time, when I returned from Germany, I had what is now known as PTSD, Post Traumatic Stress Disorder. When I arrived in Fort Dix to be discharged, I knew something was not right with me. I went to see the core man and he told me to go talk to the commander."

"Who was the core man?" Ray asked.

"It's the doctor on base. 'I'm sick!' I pleaded with him not to discharge. I wanted to get help first. 'I need help! Please, don't let me go!'

"The commander was no different, he told me, 'Well, we don't have any such thing, for what you say you have.'

"I told the officer who was discharging me, 'Something is not right with me.' I was hoping someone would listen.

"'Yeah,' he answered sarcastically, 'You smell like you've been drinking!'

"'I don't know what else to do!' I told him. But they still discharged me without any help.

"When I got home, I knew something was not right with me. My life was already different, but I didn't know exactly why. At first, it didn't seem to bother me until I started having terrifying dreams about the missions I had taken part in, especially the seventh one. I couldn't get them out of my mind. Deep inside, I had a death wish.

"Even though Abe said the park was dangerous, I welcomed the challenge, especially after hearing what the gangs were doing to innocent people.

"Before I went to the park that day, I went home and put together a makeshift ice cooler. I got a small box, attached handles to it and lined the inside with aluminum foil, then filled it with ice and a six pack of beer. I went to my room, and there in my closet, stashed away, were six guns."

"How did you get six guns?" Ray asked surprised.

"I bought them just before I had gone to visit my brothers and sisters in San Jose. I was passing by a pawn shop and saw them on sale. They were just nineteen dollars each. I even had a leather holster made special to hold all six of those guns."

"What kind of guns were they?" Ray asked.

"I don't remember, they looked like German Lugers, but weren't. They shot twenty-two caliber long shells. I hadn't planned for something like this when I bought the guns."

"Weren't you afraid of getting shot?"

"I had no fear. I was already sick, but didn't know to what extent. In the army, I was always prepared and to me this was no different."

"What happened?" Ray asked anxiously.

"I arrived at the park well before dark. I had my cooler with beer and put it on a picnic table. I sat down, opened myself a beer and then scooted the cooler behind me, real close to the edge of the picnic table. I waited patiently until nightfall. It started. From the corner of my eye I noticed about four or five guys approaching. In the hazy distance, I could see a lot more of them headed my way. Calmly, I sat there, drinking my beer with my back to them.

"Within minutes I heard the hissing sound of a beer can being popped opened, and then another, and another, until all were opened. I turned around and saw five pachucos (thugs). They were drinking my beer and taunting me with mean stares.

"'I'm not a liquor store,' I told them calmly, 'so I'm gonna charge you five bucks a can.'

"One of the guys strutted over and planted his big foot on the bench. 'Well, Èse (man), I wanna know how you're gonna collect?'

"I didn't dare take my eyes off him. He didn't notice when I slipped a hand into my coat and took out one of my guns, 'Give me my five dollars,' I demanded pointing the gun to his face.

"Surprised to be looking into the barrel of a gun, he stuttered, 'I don't have it!' I lowered the barrel to his foot and shot a round."

"You shot his foot?" Ray said surprised, "Just like that?"

"Sure did. Shocked as hell, the guy started cussing, hopping, and yelling from pain, all at the same time. I thought he was going to shit in his pants, just like that one Lieutenant on my fifth mission!

"I didn't allow my face to show any expression as I aimed the gun to his face again, then said, 'The next time … You're going to get a head shot.'

"In panic, the guy started asking his friends for money. The others who had also taken my beer, dug into their pockets, anxious to lay down their five dollars. I didn't have pity on any of them. These gangs had been hurting innocent women and children at the park, and I felt it my duty to protect them.

"Within ten minutes, I emptied three of my guns. Each clip held fourteen bullets and I didn't waste a bullet. I didn't kill anyone, but I shot each one either in the foot or hand. Most of them lay on the ground, squirming like ants sprayed with bug spray, moaning and groaning. I grabbed my cooler and left the park."

"Dad, how many of them were there?"

"Lots of them, they came out of the woodwork like ants. The next day, with the money I made from the beer, I invited Abe to dinner. When paying the cashier, I stuck my hand into my pocket to get money and some change fell on the floor. I bent down to pick it up. Wow! I saw a wad of bills lying there. I scooped it up and put it in my pocket quickly and then handed one of those bills to the cashier. I thought it was a twenty, but it wasn't, it was a hundred dollar bill.

"The cashier looked surprised at being handed a large bill, and said, 'I'll bring you the change.'

"When I got home, I pulled out the wad of bills and counted it. There was nearly nine hundred dollars. That was definitely my lucky day!"

"Dad, how did you meet mom?"

"I had dated her only once before the Army and when I got home, we started seeing each other. She was Abe's niece, but I didn't know that at the time. Your mom and I got married one month after I returned to LA from the army. I felt comfortable with her because she seemed to understand me. After dating a few weeks, I asked her to marry me.

"It had already been a week that I asked her, but she hadn't given me an answer yet. One evening after taking her home, I decided to try a different approach.

"The next day, I phoned her early and said, 'Get ready Lenora, we're going to a picnic today. I want you to wear a real pretty dress for me.' And she did, she was all dressed up when I went to pick her up. I drove up to her parent's house in my Dad's car. I opened the car door and she got in. I thought your mom was the prettiest girl I had ever seen.

"Her parent's house was up on a hill and as I drove a little ways down the hill, I pulled over and stopped. 'Lenora... let's go to TJ and get married today!'

"'Today?' she said surprised.

"'Yes,' she answered, 'but we'll have to go back and ask my mom's permission.'

"It was customary to ask your parents for their blessing, but I looked at her real serious and said, 'If we go back, then we'll never see each other again, so what's your answer?'

"Your mom knew I was serious. 'Yes!' She said. And so we drove off to TJ, Mexico and eloped; it was March 19th, 1960."

"Why did you guys get married in TJ?" Ray asked.

"In those days, the guys had to be twenty-one to marry legally. The girls could legally marry at eighteen, your mother was eighteen, but I was only twenty. That's why we had to go to Mexico to marry."

"That doesn't make sense, Dad, you were old enough to be in the army and to kill, and you weren't old enough to marry?"

"I know," I told Ray, "It was hypocritical."

"Did you go to the parks after you married mom?"

"I had no intentions of continuing my adventures in the park, but it happened. Two or three weeks after we married, I heard someone talking about a park in a different part of the city where people were complaining they couldn't go there without getting hurt. I asked a lot of questions, found out where the park was, and set out one afternoon to find it. I had worked hard all day then went over there not really prepared for anything. As soon as I walked into the park, a bunch of guys started heading towards me.

"Slowly I pressed my arms close to my ribs to feel the holster with my guns. Oh No! I had forgotten them! At first I thought about leaving real fast, but didn't.

"'Boy you better be fast today!' I told myself. 'You worked all day and now you got to fight!' I took a deep breath, remembering my old Army Sergeant's motto, *"You can take them all! If you can dance all night, you can fight all day!"* And I did. One of them came at me with an iron pipe. I took it away from him easy, and that became my weapon. None were left standing.

"For four years I went to the parks. My intentions were to get rid of the criminal element. I felt I was doing the city a favor. I justified my behavior by thinking of all those innocent people and children who were the prey of gangs. They would be safer in the end. I wanted to give them their parks back.

"At first I went just once a month, sometimes twice. Pretty soon I was going every week, on Fridays and Saturdays, to different parks around the city. In those days, most of the parks in LA were run by the gangs."

Ray nodded in agreement, "I saw a documentary the other day about the gangs in LA during that time, and you're right, the parks were infested with gangs."

Ray stood up from his chair and stretched. "Dad, I got to leave to get some supplies. I have an early job tomorrow morning. Do you think we can get back to the book in a few days?"

"Sure son." I gave Ray a hug and he left.

I felt good. Finally, after all these years, I was getting help writing my story. It seemed I had lived many lifetimes. Sometimes I could remember things very clearly and other times, I couldn't remember what I did yesterday. I used to joke with my friends that I had a condition known as CRS…. Can't Remember Shit!

I had put Lenora and my children through a lot all these years. This was the longest Lenora and I had ever lived in one place. When I was first admitted into the VA hospital in 1995, one of my counselors asked Lenora to write down every place she remembered that we had moved, and also how many jobs I had held. She counted at least thirty-five we had lived at; the jobs were even more. I led a very nomadic life, and my family was always there with me. It really helps that our sons, Willie and Ray are living with us now, otherwise, I might not be living here.

13

TWENTY DOLLARS AND A MAP

"Dirty Work"

A week later, Ray and I were back at the book, "Hey, Dad, where did you go yesterday?"

"I went to an appointment at the VA in Albuquerque, and then went to visit Andy."

"You and Andy are pretty close, aren't you?"

"I consider him family. I don't have much family left. There were eight in my family and now I only have two surviving sisters, Annabelle and Maryanne, and Paul, my half brother."

"How long has it been since your mom passed on?"

"I lost my mother in 1975, and then my father, in 1985. Andy is like a brother to me, we've been close since I met him in the PTSD group. I have no doubt in my mind that if Andy and I had met before my big flashback in 1995, we would be millionaires."

"Dad, did the police ever catch you battling with those gangs in the parks?"

"Yes, eventually I got caught. The first time the cops almost caught me, I had already cleaned up about four or five parks. I heard that a woman, her son, and daughter were beaten up and robbed the week before at this one park. I got there about eight o'clock in the evening and exercised. I practiced my jumps and shadow boxed while I waited for it to get dark. Pretty soon, people started leaving the park early.

"One man who noticed I wasn't leaving approached me real concerned and said, 'Don't stay here, it's dangerous! Leave with us please, I'll take care of you.'

"I just smiled and the more I smiled he repeated, 'I'm not lying. When it gets dark, the gangs come out!'

"The old man couldn't persuade me so finally he left. I think he was so worried for me that he may have called the cops to report a man in danger of getting really hurt. I waited by the park bench for the gangs to arrive.

"Sure enough, they came. Most of them had already been drugging and drinking. I heard someone say 'Looks like you don't want to live Ėse (man).'

"'That goes both ways!' I answered.

"They came from out of nowhere! I couldn't believe how many more came. I only expected twenty to thirty men but there were around fifty or sixty!

"To my surprise half of them were young kids between thirteen and eighteen. Some of the older ones came toward me. I waited to see if they had any kind of weapons behind their backs or in their coats.

"As soon as they got close enough, I said, 'I'm here to get even with you, for the woman and her two kids that you beat up the other day.'

"One of the men yelled at me 'What are you waiting for, let's go Ėse!'

"He came at me with a kick. I caught it in mid air with my left hand and punched him in the throat with my right. Down he went gagging immediately. Another man ran at me, I wacked him in the side of the neck and kicked him in the groin and he too went down! Then all of them came at me. I kicked and punched my way through the whole bunch and then started running.

"I ran through the park as they ran after me. I was in better shape than most of them and they couldn't catch me. I ran for about five minutes then stopped cold in my tracks, turned around, and fired kicks and punches as they came at me.

"They were easy! I was well trained and still in very good condition, I hadn't forgotten anything. Exhausted and tired the whole bunch kept coming, most of them were breathing hard. I knocked four or five down at a time and again, took off running hard for another five minutes.

"As I was running, I looked back and saw that they were too far back so I slowed down and pretended like I was tired too. When they caught up, I did the same thing - beat up another four or five."

"I bet that must have looked hilarious to someone looking at this whole scene," Ray said laughing. I nodded in agreement and started laughing too.

"I am not kidding; I might have done this to about twenty guys."

"Did the young kids beat up on you too?" Ray asked.

"Yes, at least they tried. I didn't want to hit them very hard, but there was too many, and they kept coming at me. The only way I stopped them was to throw them. I picked them up one by one and threw them on the ground like rags dolls.

"Finally, that was enough to get them to stop. The whole bunch started running away. Now it was my turn to chase them down. When I caught up to them, it became a vicious brawl. Some of the fat guys lay on the ground trying to get their wind. I grinned, easy targets! I ran and jumped on top of each one delivering more kicks and punches.

"'Don't come back to my park!' I told them, shoving my foot in their chest as they lay sprawled on the ground. 'I'm coming back here tomorrow... and maybe even the next day.... or the following week... or in a month, and if I catch or see you here.... I will follow you home and cut your head off! No one will ever know what happened!'"

"How long did you fight them?"

"The brawl lasted two to three hours, and I know I hurt some of them pretty bad. The Army taught me how to kill, not fight. I used everything I had learned - whatever it took to come out of there alive."

"What did you do after it was all over?"

"I knew I had to get out of there fast. I straightened out my clothes, wiped the sweat off my face as if nothing happened, and starting walking out of the park calmly. I heard the sound of sirens getting louder and as soon as I walked out of the park, a bunch of cop cars arrived all at once.

"A car door open behind me and a cop hollered in my direction, "Didn't you hear all that ruckus? There's a gang fight going on back there!"

"I turned around but continued to walk away; I answered him, 'Aren't you going in?'

"'No, we're waiting for back-up!'"

"'Sounds like they were afraid of the gangs?' Ray said smiling.

"It was obvious they were." I told Ray, "I was just lucky they didn't suspect I was involved. I left without being questioned or arrested.

"I was almost busted a second time. Again the cops arrived as I was leaving one of the parks. I recognized one of them, I'm pretty sure it was the same cop that stopped me the first time.

"He hollered, 'Hey, aren't you the same guy we saw at the other park?'

"'No,' I answered, I kept my head turned away, 'You must have me confused with someone else,' and I quickly disappeared down a sidewalk.

"The third time I wasn't so lucky. Someone reported gun shots and a big commotion going on in the park and cops arrived as I was trying to leave.

"'Hey!' It was the same cop, he pointed at me, 'I want to talk to you... Don't leave!' I stopped and he kept his eye on me as he walked across the street.

"He approached me slowly, "Son... do you have guns?'

"'Yes,' I answered reluctantly.

"He motioned for me to sit down with him on a bench. We both sat down at the same time.

"'Let me see them,' he muttered. Slowly, I unbuttoned the top buttons to my jacket, just enough so he could see a couple of the guns.

"'Yep, you got guns!' We both sat there in silence for a minute, I could tell he was thinking about something. 'Do you really want to get these guys?' He finally asked."

"What did you say?"

"I accepted his offer. At first, I had no intentions of cleaning up all the parks of gangs. The cops knew I had no fear, but they didn't know I had a death wish. I still couldn't sleep at night and was drinking a lot to forget the recurring nightmares and flashbacks. I thought I could ease my pain by making the parks safer for the children. Deep inside, I wanted to make things right for the innocent children that died while I was following orders in that last mission. I wanted to die, but, if someone wanted to kill me they had to earn it.

"After that last incident at the park, the cops would call on me at all hours of the night. I would meet them someplace and they would bring me a six pack of beer, a map and gas money. The map indicated the park they wanted me to go to that night. I found out quickly that the County of Los Angeles is big!

"Dad, how long did you do this?"

"Off and on for about four years. After awhile they started using me for other things besides the parks. Sometimes they came at night to my house, but most of the time, the cops would pull me over in my car and give me an address.

"This one time they gave me an address to a nightclub. They wanted me to flush out a gang member that was in the club. The plan was for me to start a fight with him, and within fifteen minutes or so, the police would then arrive and close the place down because of the brawl. They had already sent me to other nightclubs to do the same thing. Many of the nightclubs were run by gang members and the cops used me to help them close it down.

"It was a Friday night. I parked a block down the street in case I had to make a quick get away from the club. This was a big nightclub. I walked through the front doors and went to the bar and asked for a beer. Then, I casually walked around with my beer looking at everybody. I made my way to the back room; it was a big room with six tables. Men dressed in suits and sport jackets were seated and eating their dinner.

"I recognized the man I was to target and walked up to his table. He was eating and talking to the others at the table and it appeared like he was their leader.

"There was a big bowl of spaghetti in the middle of the table and I casually reached into the bowl with my bare hands and got a handful of spaghetti and began to eat it. I just looked at them, smiled, and took a drink of my beer then put my glass down on the table and cleaned my hands on a nice suit jacket hanging on the back of a chair. I could have used one of their cloth napkins, but I didn't. I wanted to make them real mad."

"Didn't anyone do anything?" Ray asked in disbelief.

"I think I caught them by surprise, they didn't know what to make of it just then. They all sat there watching what I was doing. There was also a cake on the table; again, with my bare hand, I grabbed a big piece and started eating it. I took another drink of my beer, glanced at them and smiled. I finally made them real mad!

"Everyone stood up all at one time, including the boss, my target. He looked impressive in his blue pinstriped suit. The man looked about fifty years old, to me that was old, since I was only twenty-three then. The men looked at him, then looked at me, and back at him, waiting for a signal. I knew everyone was anxious to beat me up.

"Then, in a firm voice, he spoke. 'Sit down everyone … nobody make a move on this man.' He then sat down and kept his eyes on me. Cautiously, he continued, 'he is either very sick…. or crazy, or… he knows he can kick our asses.'

"Before he could finish the last sentence, one of his men pulled out a gun and pointed it at me. I took it out of his hand before he knew what happened. The old man quickly stood up again, and everyone jumped up too. He repeated……

He repeated, "'I said! Don't start a fight with this man!

Even if he hurts or tries to shoot me! Understand! Or I personally will shoot you!'

"All this time he didn't take his eyes off me. Calmly he said to me, 'Eat anything you want son. Get a plate and order a drink. Sit anywhere you want.'

"He then sat back down slowly and all his men did the same. I picked up my beer from the table and walked back to the bar and sat down on a stool.

"Instinctively, I knew it was exactly ten o'clock. I didn't have to look at a clock. As in past similar scenarios, the cops came abruptly through the front doors expecting a big mess. As soon as they came into the nightclub, they walked around asking everyone if they were okay. While they were busy doing this, one of the cops came discreetly over to where I was sitting.

"He looked at me bothered, obviously mad. In a low voice he asked, 'What happened.... You were supposed to start a fight.'

"I looked at him and smiled, 'I tried... What can I say?' I got up and left. This was the last time I went to do their dirty work at nightclubs, but I still did other things for them.

"I didn't mind helping them out, but I didn't like some of things they wanted me to do. And if I didn't cooperate, they threatened bringing me in for my lawless activities."

"Lawless activities..." Ray said in disbelief.

"Yes," I answered, "Even though most of the lawless activities were things they initiated. This went on for another three years."

"So when did it all stop?"

"Well, one day Charles, a good friend of my two older brothers, came to visit them from Oakland. That evening I was headed out to one of the parks, but first, I stopped at their house to visit for a little while. My brothers worked at night and they were getting ready to leave, so Charles asked if he could come with me. He had no idea what I was up to. At first I was hesitant but said okay.

"When we got to the park I told him, 'Wait for me in the car, I'll be back.'

"'No, I want to go with you.'

"'I think you better stay here, you might get hurt or even worse....get killed.'

"'I can take care of myself,' he said confidently.

"'We might have to get into a fight.'

"'Like I said, I can take care of myself.' Charles was not prepared for what was coming down.

"How can you do this?" Charles asked me after the brawl. I told him who had sent me there.

"Are they paying you a lot of money?"

"'No, I don't get paid anything."

"He looked at me dismayed.

"Well then… how much do you make in construction?"

"I make $3.50 an hour."

"Listen Frank, this is dangerous, what you do. Come work for me in Oakland, I can pay you $3.50 an hour too. Be at my plating shop in two weeks. You said you know the business, right?" I nodded yes.

"I went home that evening and told Lenora 'Let's move! I want to get far away from LA. I have a job waiting for me at Burlingame Plating, in Oakland and I have to be at work in two weeks.'"

14

THE PLATING BUSINESS

"Back Breaking Work"

"Dad, you told your friend Charles you knew how to plate, when did you learn that?"

"The reason I knew about the plating business is because my brothers had taught me about it when I was about thirteen years old. My older brothers, Ben and Willie, worked at 101 Plating in San Jose. I used to go with them to work and help around the shop.

"The owner, Ed Englehart, took a liking to me. He always treated me and my brothers really good. He took me under his wing and taught me a lot about plating, even mixing the chemicals. Actually, he showed me everything he knew about mixing all the chemicals and I soaked it all up. I didn't forget anything he taught me.

"Then, when I came home from the Army in 1960, one of the many jobs I had, was for Faith Plating in Hollywood, California. I worked there for about four to six months. I had so many jobs I can't remember exactly how long I worked for them.

"When I went to work for Charles at Burlingame Plating in Oakland, we stayed with my brother Ben in Milpitas for about two months, until we rented a house down the street from him. They started me as an apprentice and in no time, I became a journeyman.

"During the time I was working for Burlingame Plating, I started going to school to learn how to become a plating chemist. The school was located in San Francisco.   I worked in Oakland by day, and after work drove to uptown San Francisco for school. I did this two hours a night for nearly a year.

"About a month after I started attending the school, the instructor quit and they couldn't find a replacement. In the meantime, everyone basically had to teach themselves from the books.

"I remembered a lot of the stuff Ed had taught me so I started helping the guys who were also taking the class and pretty soon I found myself teaching the class. They couldn't find an instructor but they didn't want to cancel the class either. I would read a book in one sitting."

"How did you do that Dad?"

"I could read real fast. I flipped through two to three pages at a time and remembered everything and would then teach it to the rest of the guys. The school noticed what I was doing and when the course finished, they offered me a job, but I turned it down. The sad thing about this was everyone in the class got a diploma for completing the school except for me."

"That doesn't make sense, did that get you mad?"

"I was upset for a while but in the end I didn't care, I knew the stuff. I didn't need a piece of paper to tell me that.

"I commuted to Burlingame Plating in Oakland for nearly a year and eventually left. I got a job with another one of Faith Plating's shops in San Jose.

"I really hadn't thought about buying a house but my brother Ben urged me to and with my wages at Faith Plating, I qualified, it was a four bedroom house with a double garage and big yard.

"I had been working for Faith Plating for about a year when I had a terrible accident, I broke my back. The wood on the catwalk I was standing on had rotted from the moisture and acid in the tanks. I was taking a bumper out of a sulfuric acid tank when the catwalk collapsed. I fell backwards real hard and hit another tank. A sharp excruciating pain instantly raced throughout my back.

"'Are you alright Frank?' the foreman asked me.

"'I think I twisted my back.' I was shaken up badly and went home. The next morning I couldn't move. My boys were in school and remembered that time clearly."

"That was the time you couldn't work for a whole year. You were in bad shape, Dad."

"I know, your mom applied for public assistance and because I couldn't provide for all of you, we qualified for aid for needy children. There was no way I could work. I couldn't even drive a car. The only solution was to have my back operated on. That type of operation was not common in those days and the cost was way up there, and I didn't have that kind of money.

"Everyday my condition worsened. I found different ways to numb the pain. I began to have frequent nightmares and flashbacks from the missions. The guilt, especially from the last mission, was just eating me up. As the days passed, I found myself in a deep depression. I was over eating and drinking too much. I gained an enormous amount of weight."

"I remember you could hardly walk," Ray added.

"Yes, that was one of the worse times of my life. Do you remember what I used to do when I wanted to visit my brother Ben, down the street?"

Ray laughed, "I do. You used to tie our dog, Whitie, with a rope to our wagon and he would pull you over to Uncle Ben's house and back."

159

"I didn't want you guys to see me real depressed so I covered it up pretty good. But, I couldn't see myself living like this.

"One day I staggered to my room and loaded my one shot forty-four magnum gun. I sat on the edge of the bed looking down its barrel for a long time and raised it slowly as I opened my mouth. I held it there for a moment then pulled the trigger, 'Click…' Sweat was rolling down my face. I couldn't understand what just happened, so I looked in the chamber and the bullet was there. I could see where the firing pin had hit the cap."

"I guess it wasn't your time… right?"

"I guess it wasn't!"

"There was a social worker for Aid for Needy Children that would come and see how the family was doing.

"She could see I wasn't doing too well. 'Mr. Wiggins, have you found a doctor who could help you?'

"'Yes,' I answered right away, 'but the doctors want to charge me sixty thousand dollars and the insurance from Faith Plating will only pay twelve thousand.'

"She shook her head in disbelief and said, 'Give me the name of the doctors and let me see what I can find out.'

"A couple of days later she gave me a call, 'Mr. Wiggins, I'm mailing a letter to you today. When you receive it, take it to your doctors. It looks like they owe the State one hundred thousand dollars.' She told me later that the doctor's had over-billed the State for some previous stuff. 'Show them the letter and you can have your operation.'

"Wow! What a blessing, my wife's prayers were answered. I was fortunate that the doctor who performed the surgery was very good and the operation was successful.

"I had to learn to walk again. The healing was slow, it didn't help that I had lost so much weight.

"Even my father was concerned about my weight loss, he told me, "Mi hijíto, pareces un viejíto (my son, you are so thin you look like an old man)."

"A little after the operation I negotiated a settlement with Faith Plating's insurance company. I didn't have a lawyer but the settlement included an understanding that I could return to my job as soon as I recuperated. I was promised some kind of job at the shop. That never happened. Five months later, I tried to return to work, but they refused to hire me.

"I was walking but hadn't regained all my flexibility. The healing was not coming fast enough. I was still drinking a lot and after Faith Plating refused to hire me back; it got worse.

"My nightmares and depression escalated. I had reached another breaking point. Since I returned from the military, I always kept several guns and rifles at home. That day, no one was home. I got one of the rifles and went to the living room. I got a white sheet and very carefully covered the sofa with it. I didn't want to ruin the furniture for my wife. Then I sat down on the sofa with my rifle. I don't know how long I sat there, but it seemed like a long while. Slowly, I lifted the loaded rifle and inserted the barrel into my mouth. I had just begun to squeeze the trigger when I heard the front door open.

"Quickly, I covered the rifle with the sheet, and heard, 'Hi, Dad, we're home.' Again, it wasn't my time!

"Deep inside I wanted to get back at Faith Plating for not making good on their agreement with me. I had to restrain myself from all the bad thoughts I was having. I had five thousand dollars left from the settlement and decided to invest it in my own plating shop; I would name it, "Bonus Plating." The thought of opening my own shop motivated me. It kept me focused on what was important in my life and one of those things was to become a fierce competitor of Faith Plating and squash them!

"My two brothers were ready to be partners."

"I thought you had three partners."

"At first it was Ben, my oldest brother, and Willie, the second to the oldest, then our friend, John, joined us. John wasn't related to us but he was always with us so we called him our brother. Even with the five thousand, I needed more money to invest in the business to really make it work, so I decided to sell our house. When I finally sold the house, I was shocked. I didn't know that the State was going to collect all the money they had helped my family with during the time I was injured. After the sale, I only made four thousand dollars.

"It took two years for Bonus Plating to start making enough money. After that, the plating shop was very successful. We chromed everything from bumpers, car rims, motorcycle parts, car parts, and specialty work for Hewlett Packard, FMC (Food Machinery Corporation), and several other big businesses.

"By the third year, we had twenty-five employees working the day shift and eight people working the night shift. We had so much business that we had three delivery trucks going from eight o'clock in the morning until about eight at night. We opened Bonus Plating in 1968 and by the end of 1970; we had more work than we could ever want.

"One day this man came to the shop looking for a job, he had only one arm. I didn't know at first that he was a veteran.

"'What happened to your arm?' I asked.

"He didn't answer at first then said, 'I lost it in Vietnam, it was blown off."

"'I'm a veteran too,' I told him. 'What are you doing here? What can I help you with?'

"'Well, I'm looking for a job.'

"'What do you think you can do here?' He shrugged his shoulders. 'Come on,' I told him, 'Let's take a look around the shop.' We looked around but every job required the use of two arms, two hands, and two legs.

"'I just need a job for about two or three days.' I heard the desperation in his voice, "I just need to make enough to go home. I spent the money they gave me drinking.'

"I know… I understand,' I said, 'but, what can you do?' 'I can sweep this place clean from one end to the other. If I don't do a good job, you don't have to pay me.'

"'Okay… then you need to get started. You got three days to clean this place.'"

"I went to the office after showing him to the cleaning supply room. Talking to him sent me back in time. I remembered when I first got out of the Army I didn't have any money either. I, too, drank to forget the nightmares and, I didn't get home until a month after my discharge.

"At the end of the three days, I paid him his money. 'I'll take you to the train station,' I told him and he accepted. After parking the car we both entered the station and walked up to the ticket window.

"'How much is the ticket?' he asked, and reached into his pocket to pay.

"'I'll pay for it,' I said, before he could take out his money.

"'No!' He replied, 'No….you don't have to do that….you did enough for me already.'

"'And you gave a lot for us!' I insisted, 'I'll pay for the ticket.' He finally let me pay and I made sure he got on the train.

"Coincidentally, one week later, another man came into the shop looking for a job. That one I put to work as an apprentice polisher. He worked for about two weeks and then told me the job was too hard.

"'Do you think I could work for only one more week? By then I'll have enough money to go home. I haven't been home. I was in Vietnam for two years and was wounded. All I want to do now is to just go home.'"

"'Of course… I understand.' He worked one more week and I paid him his money; I even gave him a bonus.

"I don't know how word got around about me helping out veterans."

Ray started laughing and said, "I remember you talking about that."

"I think they put a mark on the front of my place or on the street advertising that I gave jobs to veterans, because a lot of guys began coming to the shop asking me for a job, money, or some kind of help. And the more I helped, the more money we made. That year my shop made over one million dollars."

"How long did you have Bonus Plating Dad?"

"I opened Bonus Plating in 1968 and walked away from it in 1973. I didn't know I was sick, I had never heard of PTSD. I had three partners, but I was the one who negotiated the most profitable contracts. Even though the business prospered, I still had nightmares and flashbacks.

"Eventually the stress and challenging situations my partners were putting me in began to take its toll. I got tired of cleaning up their messes. I gave my partners four months notice that I was leaving. They pleaded for me to stay, but I had already made up my mind.

"'Make sure you pay the quarterly taxes on time and don't forget to transfer the business to your names as soon as possible.' I took my share of the profits and put enough money into an account for the quarterly taxes before I left."

15

THE PROJECTS

"Living in a Third World Country"

"I moved my family to Santa Fe, New Mexico and went to live with my wife's mother until I could find us a place. I had about one hundred thousand dollars from the plating business and when we got to Santa Fe, I deposited it in a bank. I used a little of the money to open up a small plating shop outside of town. This guy in Pojoaque was going out of business and he gave me a great deal on everything.

"All the while I felt good because I had a nest egg in the bank. Six months passed and I went to my bank to take out some money. I was shocked; it was all gone. My partners hadn't paid their quarterly taxes and they also hadn't removed my name from the business contract. The IRS took everything! All I could afford to do was to rent a small one bedroom apartment for my big family.

"Again I became restless and before long, I moved us back to Los Angeles. I began doing construction work for the oil refineries. By 1976, my wife and I had five children. Vivian was our oldest and our four younger boys were Frankie, Louie, Willie, and Ray. I had saved enough money working construction and had purchased a truck. I was now self-employed.

"When the business began to slow down, I decided to sell my hauling truck and move the family once again to Santa Fe, New Mexico. My wife kept track of the times we moved. From the day I was discharged from the Army in 1960, this was the twenty-sixth time.

"My family wanted me to be the way I was before, but I was not the same person. I thought that I could forget what had happened to me in Germany, but I got worse as time went by.

"If I didn't have a few drinks, I couldn't go to sleep. I was drinking more and more with each passing day. Everything seemed to bother me. The neighborhood noises, car doors slamming, people talking, dogs barking, cats crying.

"I was getting more irritable as the years went by. I would get angry for nothing. I was making life harder for my family and making it harder for them to cope with me. I had dozens and dozens of jobs, but I couldn't keep them for very long. I moved my family back and forth, from city to city and state to state and finally ended up in Santa Fe, New Mexico.

"The intense training I had in the army stayed with me throughout the years and as the years passed, I became hypersensitive and vigilant. I was constantly suspicious of anyone and everyone. I couldn't be around people. When I went to a restaurant or was somewhere doing business, I sat with my back to the wall, and most of the time, I carried a weapon.

"At night I would check the doors and windows for possible intruders. For sixteen years, I worked out two hours a night. Those who dared to invade my territory never forgot my punishment. The trauma that I experienced during the missions in Germany still continued to plague me. The nights were bad, sleepless and full of nightmares.

"When I got to New Mexico, I was making more money drawing unemployment from California, than if I worked. Everybody wanted to hire me, but they only wanted to hire me part-time. I would have lost my benefits if I accepted part-time employment. I weighed my options and decided to stay home and take care of my little baby girl Jaime who had just been born. My wife went to work as a seamstress and worked eight hour days, five days a week.

"This situation didn't last too long. I was starting to get restless, but I enjoyed staying home with the baby. I talked to Jaime every day as if she was an adult.

"'Say mama, can you say mama?' I repeated it over and over and then to my surprise she said it…. 'Ma…ma,' Jaime was only six months old, it freaked me out! That day when my wife got home from work I excitedly told her the baby had started talking.

"'No way, stop making it up,' she said in disbelief.

"I got her by the arm and took her over to Jaime's crib, 'Really, it's true! Come and listen. 'Jaime, Say mama' and she did. At the age of seven months, Jamie was a chatter box. She absorbed everything on TV, books and conversations. She was a very smart little girl. I remember my mother saying I had done similar things. I used to have a photographic memory. Maybe she was taking after me. Now I have C. R. S. (Can't Remember Shit!).

"Finally, I got a chance to earn some good money. A cousin of mine offered to sell me his dump truck, and that's how I became owner operator of a GMC ten wheel dump truck. I was doing pretty good, hauling everything. Sometimes my jobs took me as far south as Ruidoso and surrounding counties. I stayed in town for a while and then I got a contract with the city of Santa Fe, it paid $18 hour. The city was widening the river downtown and a bunch of trucks were hired to remove the gravel and debris from the river. One day I was parked on the corner of Alameda and

Saint Francis Street, waiting for my turn for them to fill my truck with gravel.

"I looked across the street and saw the projects for the first time. For a second it reminded me of some parts of Germany after the war except without all the graffiti. The apartment walls were worn and covered with graffiti. Trash, dirty diapers, newspapers, every kind of debris you could think of, was scattered all over the place.

"I glanced to the entrance of the projects, and on the wall in big letters someone had sprayed with silver paint, 'ENTER AT YOUR OWN RISK.'

"I thought to myself, 'My God, who can live there! They should send somebody to clean that whole place and throw out all the bad people that caused that mess!' The line started moving, so I started up my truck and went back to work.

"I worked all over the city for about two more months and then someone who had it out for me put sugar in my truck's motor oil. Not one time, but four times."

"Do you know who did it?" Ray asked.

"Yes, but that's another story. Anyway, between fixing my truck and business slowing down, I couldn't keep up the truck payments. It got so bad that I went bankrupt. To make matters worse, the landlord said he was moving back into his house so he needed us to move out. Now I became in desperate need of a home.

***This is where my story began in the projects;
crossing the border from one way of life into another.***

170

"In desperation, I went to the housing authorities to apply for housing. From there, they sent me to see a man named Rick Marez. I had a hard time finding the office and finally found it. I sat down in the waiting room with a bunch of other people. Sitting there, I overheard some of his workers refer to him as Tomcat, and then they started laughing. I must have waited 15 to 20 minutes before it was my turn to enter his office.

"'Hello', he shook my hand, 'I'm Rick Marez, and you're Mr. Wiggins, right?'

"'Yes sir,' I replied.

"'I'm sorry to tell you Mr. Wiggins, but we don't have any houses available. We already have a long waiting list.' I explained to him my desperate situation.

"'Listen… I just went bankrupt and the landlord just told me he needs the house we're living in. Tomcat… if you can do anything to help me, I would surely appreciate it.'

"I noticed his face turned real red as soon as I called him Tomcat.

"'Who told you my name was Tomcat?'

"'Isn't that what they call you?' He got angry and responded, 'I got somewhere you can live! I have a house nobody else wants…do you want it?'

"'Yes, I'll take it!' I thanked him. I was just relieved to have a place to take my family.

"One of the city workers took Lenora and me to see the house. It wasn't a house, it was an apartment, and it was in real bad condition. It looked abandoned with the windows all boarded up. Lenora and I looked at each other as the man took us inside. It was as cold as a walk-in freezer.

"My wife and I looked at each other again. It wasn't much, but since we needed to move out of the other house right away, we both knew this had to do. 'We'll take it!' I said.

"'Do you want the boards to stay on the windows?'

"I thought that was a strange question. 'No…. my wife likes the sun to come in,' and before moving in that day, Lenora and I went to the Welfare Office to try and get some help.

"We felt we had contributed to the community every place we had ever lived. We paid our share of taxes. We had never asked for help except when I broke my back. Even then, the state collected everything they gave us when we sold our home. Both of us felt we were entitled for some help.

"To our surprise, they denied us the help we needed. Lenora and I left their office very angry. They said we did not qualify for assistance.

"'Maybe,' they said, 'you might be eligible for food stamps.'

"We didn't have any time to linger on our frustration. We went to our house and loaded up the truck. When we got to the apartment with our first load of furniture, the city workers had already taken off the boards. Lenora was happy to see we now had a nice big window.

"I looked around at the other apartments in our area; their windows were boarded up. 'How strange,' I thought, 'people are still living in them.' I had no idea how bad things really were in the projects.

"After my boys and I moved everything into our new place, I went outside to wait for my friend, Eddie, to come pick up the truck I had borrowed. The day was chilly from the snow the day before and today it was cloudy. I was enjoying the warmth from the late evening's sun's rays.

"Before I knew it, three young men approached me and one of them said, 'You better move out now... unless you and your family want to get hurt!'

"On the ground was a wooden stake. I calmly picked it up and with it drew a circle around my apartment, five feet from the wall. 'You see this circle? No one is allowed within this circle after dark... and if anyone even comes within one foot of it... I will catch them. No matter where they run to, I will catch them!' I know I caught them off guard, I don't think they expected to be intimidated, and they all left in a hurry.

"That first night was quiet; so quiet you could almost hear a pin drop. The following night, about ten o'clock, it began. They came in pairs. When I moved into the projects, I never tried to start a fight, but I never ran from one either. These guys came looking for a fight. They wanted to claim what they thought was theirs. I didn't care if harm came to me, but to my family, that was unacceptable.

"On this particular night, a couple of them tried to sneak up on me. I was already outside quietly waiting with my black German shepherd, Jethro. Quietly I waited with Jethro at my side.

"Before they knew it, I was right in front of them. I startled the two and one of the guys threw a punch. Without hesitation, I punched the first one hard in the face and elbowed the one behind him in the chest. I then punched the first one again and kicked the second one on the head. As they lay bloodied on the ground, I walked up to each individually and stood on their chests with my foot.

"I lifted my foot and pressed down real hard on their face and said, 'You'd better not come back to my place!' As soon as I let them get up they ran off limping."

"Dad," Ray asked, "Remember the time you were coming home from the pizza place and those guys from the projects tried to beat you up?"

"Yes, that was about a week after we moved in. I was having a hard time because my unemployment hadn't kicked in yet. I had no job, no money, had applied for food stamps but they turned us down. They said we didn't qualify because I should have saved the money I made from the sale of my truck in California.

"I was at home moping and doing nothing. My oldest daughter, Vivian, had moved out on her own, she was barely sixteen. Vivian worked at a Pizza Hut in town and called to ask me if I wanted some pizza and beer.

"'Of course,' I said.

"'Okay, Dad,' Vivian said, 'bring a big pitcher for the beer.'

"She made my day. The Pizza Hut was only five blocks away and so I walked over to her work with my empty pitcher. Sure enough, Vivian fixed me up. She loaded me up with pizza, filled my pitcher with beer, and I went walking home with a smile on my face.

"Umm.... the smell of pizza made me real hungry so when I reached the Salvation Army building, I stopped to have some pizza while it was still hot and also take a drink of cold beer. I sat down on the big front steps of the Salvation Army building.

"Right then this guy came running from the side of the building taunting me to fight. From the other side of the building came another guy, he had a sniff rag in one hand, a beer in the other. Both of these guys looked stupid, they had been sniffing paint.

"I put my pizza and beer down, but not before taking a drink of beer. Immediately these guys were taking swings at me. It was like fighting two kids. In no time, I beat the hell out of them and they ran to the back of the building like dogs with tails between their legs.

"I sat down on the steps again and took a bite of pizza and another drink of beer. I couldn't believe it; two more guys came out from the back of the building, kicking and swinging at me. I beat them up too. Three more guys came out and they too met the same fate. I ate a little more pizza, took another drink of beer, and got ready to leave. I couldn't believe it!

"Where were all these guys coming from? In all, there must have been about twenty that I beat up. Finally, I sat down and drank some more beer.

"This older lady walked over from one of the units at the senior citizen housing projects next door, she asked, 'Are you guys making a movie? Where's the camera?'

"'No, lady, this is not a movie,' I said laughing, 'This is real life!'

"She laughed. 'You fight pretty good! I seen those kicks and punches, it sure looked like a movie.'

"I picked up the pizza box and pitcher of beer, smiled and continued on my way home."

"Dad, why do you think they wanted to beat you up so bad?"

"They were used to having their way with everyone in the projects and when they found out they couldn't intimidate me, they didn't like it.

"A week went by and during that time I didn't see my wife very much. My wife is a Jehovah witness and sometimes after work, she would do her Christian work after the word service.

"One particular night, after we had all gone to bed, I heard someone knock on my living room window. 'Who's there?' I asked.

"I heard a voice answer, 'I'm waiting for you outside man…let's take care of business.'

"I already knew what he wanted. I armed myself with a bat and snuck outside through the back door. As I rounded the corner, I saw a man standing by the staircase. He was a Hispanic dude, about a head taller than me and very muscular. When he saw me, he began twirling nun chucks, around his neck and around his waist.

"I kept my eyes on him as he twirled them. I noticed that the only time his eyes left me was when he twirled the nun chucks around his leg. So I waited and waited for him to make a mistake.

"'I'm going to beat the shit out of you!' He kept telling me.

"And then it happened, he took his eyes off me for a split second as he twirled the nun chucks around his leg. I swung my bat and hit him on the side of the head. I gave him four more home runs.

"He put his hand out, 'Please… don't hit me anymore… Please… no more!' He begged and pleaded.

"'Get out of here and don't come back again!' He got up and starting walking away. He looked at his nun chucks; they were lying on the ground.

"'Take them with you! Hang them over your right wrist and put that hand in your back pocket. Put your other hand in your front pocket and you better not make any sudden moves!'

"The guy took a few steps and turned his head real fast, as if he was going to try and come back at me. That was a mistake! Before he could completely turn around, I hit him in back of the head with the bat, "POW!" He landed on the dirt. I heard noise and looked up. We had an audience of maybe 200 people. They were standing in the shadows where I couldn't see them too well.

"The gang members had actually hired a professional to get me, but it didn't work. After that, things were quiet and safe, but only for a while.

"My dog, Jethro, was my partner. I guarded my home at night and slept during the day and I had him trained to alert me when someone was nearby. The apartment complex we lived in was an eight-plex - four apartments upstairs and four downstairs. If you faced the building, our apartment was located on the right bottom side next to a staircase. There was constant partying at night and people gathered on the stairs, in the hallway, between the apartments, and on the balcony.

"My wife had to get up real early for work and she couldn't sleep with all the noise. Finally, one night about one o'clock in the morning, she asked me to tell them not to be so noisy. I was angry too because it was like this every night. I kept a machete and baseball bat by my front door. I got my machete and went outside through the back door. I walked all the way to the front of the building with the machete hidden behind my leg and Jethro at my side.

"I approached quietly and stood at the bottom of the staircase, there was about thirty girls and boys.

"I yelled… 'I want everyone to leave! That's my staircase you're on!'

"They weren't fazed; they just cussed and yelled back, 'the stairs aren't yours!' I pulled out the machete from the back of my leg and made sure they could see it in the moonlight.

"Again I yelled out, 'Whoever does not leave right now is going to leave in a plastic bag! Jethro!' I yelled, and he lunged toward them growling, his white canines ready to bite.

"'Éste vato está loco!' (This guy is crazy), I overheard someone say. I waived the machete back and forth slightly and all of them scattered.

"'Don't come back to my place!'

"We were happy when new neighbors moved in above us and also across the street. They both took the boards off their windows and pretty soon, the rest of the neighbors did the same."

"Dad, remember the time they shot into our apartment?"

"I sure do," I answered.

"How old was I?"

"You were about fourteen."

Ray prompted me to stop for a second so he could replace the batteries in the digital recorder. "Okay, keep going."

"My children lived through many of my escapades and I am so grateful none of them ever got hurt. A month passed without anymore major events with the gangs. Then, one evening, the whole family was sitting around the living room watching TV. We were munching on goodies and just enjoying ourselves.

"All of a sudden we heard gunshots and realized someone was shooting at our house. Bullets hit the door and the outside wall. I ran to the front door and flung it open, a black car was pulling away and I was able to see four people inside, they were shooting at me as the car sped off. I kept a rifle by the door so I grabbed it and started shooting back.

"As soon as I started firing, my older son, Frankie, Jr., knew what to do. He immediately ran to the room and brought me more ammunition. My aim was good and I had no doubt I hit one of them.

"The next day I was talking to the neighbor and saw a guy with a cast on his leg.

"'What happened to that guy?'"

"'Oh, someone said he was shot the other night.'"

"That must have been the one you shot, Right?"

"Yes" I answered. I never did anything they didn't deserve."

"Wasn't it after this that the neighborhood nicknamed you, "El heavy Loco?"

I laughed, "Yes."

16

EL HEAVY LOCO

"One Punch Kill"

"One day a man from the city housing office came to my apartment. I didn't remember getting a notice he was coming.

"'Hello, Mr. Wiggins, I'm an inspector for the City Housing Authority.' I let him enter then he asked, 'Is the neighborhood quiet at night around here?'

"'Yes,' I responded. As he asked, his eyes were scanning my living room. He could see all the tools I had by the door; my bat, rifle and machete.

"Ray, I remember you were listening to our conversation, and blurted out, 'My dad goes out and plays baseball every night.'

"The inspector looked at me and said, 'I've been looking for someone like you... I want you to go with me to see Jerry Davey, he's the housing director. He might have a job opening for you.'

"That sounded great to me, 'Okay, I could use a job,' I answered. The following morning I went to the City Housing Office to meet Jerry Davey.

"As I entered Jerry Davey's office I heard a voice say, 'Hello, Mr. Wiggins. He walked over from behind his desk, 'I've heard a lot about you. I could use a man with your skills.' I shook his hand and he asked, 'Would you like to start work for us in the maintenance department?'

"Being I was without a job, I quickly replied, 'Yes, sir.'

"'Good…I was hoping you would say that. I want you to go downtown to the unemployment office and ask for a man named Armijo. He'll take care of you.'

"And so I did. I was enrolled into the C.I.T.A. program as a temporary worker for the City Housing Authority doing maintenance work at the projects. It helped that I was a veteran because veterans got hiring preference. I was a probationary worker for a few months and then on July 1st, 1979, I became a permanent employee.

"I was real happy at the end of that day. I finished my work at one of the housing projects and went home walking. I was already half way home when I heard a honk. It was George Ramirez. George was the inspector for the housing, but he was also in charge of all maintenance. He pulled over and offered me a ride home.

"It was George who told me what to do. Every morning I would pick up the day's work schedule from him. Up to now, all he had me doing was painting, cutting grass, and cleaning yards. There were three locations in Santa Fe that had housing projects, and I was doing work at all of them.

"Before we got to my house, George stopped at Walgreen's to pick up a six-pack of cokes. When we got to my house, we parked in the parking lot in front of the apartment building.

"George took a drink of his coke then said, 'Frank, there's a lot of room for advancement working for housing, but you have to work hard to get it. I've been watching you, and you learn quickly. You know how to take orders and how to give orders. That's a big plus for you, Frank.'

"As we were having our conversation two men drove up in a red station wagon and parked right next to our car. Both men got out and ran up the stairs to the apartment above mine. They were inside for just about five minutes, then we saw the apartment door swing open and out they came.

"Both of them ran down the stairs and then walked up to George's car. They looked shifty.

"One of them leaned forward and propped his hands on George's car door and said, 'Hey man, are you the inspector for the city housing?'

"'Yes,' George replied.

"'We're police, and you men are not supposed to be drinking in government vehicles.'

"George looked over at me. He was thinking the same thing I was; these guys didn't notice we were drinking cokes.

"'Frank…' George said, 'Can you get down and get the license plate number from their car.'

"Without hesitation, I got out and walked to the back of their car and wrote their license plate number on a piece of paper. While I was doing this, one of the men came around the back of the car and threw a punch at me. I stopped his fist in mid air and fired several hard punches. Down he went! His friend ran to help him. He tried to hit me, but I blocked his punch too and hit him one time with all my might... that was it for him. His partner got up and tried to come at me again. He reached for something in his back pocket. I thought it was a knife.

"George yelled out, 'Take it easy Frank, they may really be cops!'

"It was too late, I had already floored him. In fact, I knocked out all his pretty front gold teeth. "I turned around just in timc to see this real big man coming from behind me.

"I was prepared to let him have it too, but then he said, 'Thank you, for not killing my son.' He reached down to the ground to help his son, the toothless guy. The man looked at his son sternly and said, 'Con los hombres no se fúegan!' (You don't play with real men). The son refused to take his father's helping hand."

Ray had been listening intently, nodding his head because he was there that day and remembered some of the events.

I asked him, "Do you remember what happened next?"

"I sure do, when I saw you fighting I was inside the house, and I ran and got your machete."

"Why did you do that?"

"Mom was inside and saw what was going on… She was scared and worried you would get hurt, so she told me to take it to you."

"It's a good thing I didn't take it... Remember? I sent you back in the house just before the real cops arrived. About how old were you son?"

Ray answered, "I was about 13 or 14."

"Just after you ran into the apartment, a swarm of police cars arrived. There must have been about four or five cars. The policemen got off their cars and looked around.

"'What's going on here?'

"George Ramirez pointed to the guys on the ground, 'These guys say they're cops.'

"The cops helped the two guys up and told them, 'Why don't you wait for us over here,' and pointed by the front of my house.

"George explained to the police what happened, 'I'm the inspector for the housing and we were just sitting here in the car.

This is my employee Mr. Wiggins and we were talking when these two guys came up and began some trouble. They said they were cops!'

"I walked toward the back of George's car and was just standing there waiting to see what the police were going to do. George was in the front of the car, I could hear what the police were telling him.

"'These guys aren't cops… they're a couple of thugs.'

"I heard sirens and then an ambulance arrived. The paramedics began checking the two guys I beat up. I guess their injuries weren't severe enough, because the ambulance left without them.

"'Do you want us to take them to jail?' One of the cops asked George.

"George looked at me, 'It's up to you Frank, are you going to press charges?'

"'No.' I answered him.

"'I'll see you tomorrow Frank.' George said as he turned around and left.

"One of the cops walked over to me and asked, 'You live here?'

"'Yes,' I said.

"'Aren't you afraid to live here?'

"When he asked me this, he got real close to me. I kept a straight face. I knew he suspected I was the one battling the gangs and cleaning up the projects.

"He shook my hand, 'Anything we can do to help you out… Just call.' And then they all left.

"The next day I went to work early. I always reported to the housing office on St. Francis and Alta Vista to get my work orders for the day.

"As I punched in, George Ramirez walked up to me and said, 'Jerry wants to see you.'

"My first thought was, 'You did it this time, Frank! Oh shit… I'm going to be fired, and just as I had gotten hired.' I know Jerry was getting complaints from gang member's families living in the projects. Jerry sensed I was the one beating up and manhandling all the hítos (sons) in the neighborhood.

"I opened the door to Jerry's office and George was already there. I knew Jerry was someone that could not be bought. He was a man with real honor and dignity. Later I found out he retired from the Marines as a 1st Sergeant.

"When I entered the room, Jerry motioned for me to sit down. 'I heard what you did yesterday, Frank. I want to offer you a job…. as security.'

"'What a relief,' I thought, 'I'm not getting fired!'

"Jerry continued, 'Although we don't have any money for you at this time, as soon as we get more funding, we can pay you. If you accept, you will oversee security for all the city housing, and any other housing that the city and HUD owns.' Jerry looked me in the eye and asked, 'Will you accept the job?'

"'Yes,' I answered. 'Then put your left hand on this book (the Bible), and your raise right hand.' I only remember saying, *'I will do my job to the very best of my ability.'*

"I took my job seriously. I was there to protect the tenants from the gangs and to help them in any way I could, but it was a very big job! Many times I had to go to Jerry Davey for more help, and if he wasn't around, to his second and third in command,

George Ramirez and Rick Marez. Finally, they gave me someone who could really help me, someone who wasn't afraid. His name was 'Lucky.'

"The first time I met Lucky was on a City Housing job. The Housing foreman had picked me and a few other guys to go work at the Cerro Gordo Flats Apartments to cut lawns and clean trash.

"Lucky was one of those guys we picked up, but he and I didn't know each other at the time. After an hour of working, my lawn mower gave out and right after that, Lucky's lawn mower broke too. The machines were already malfunctioning and finally, the engines just blew.

"'What do you think?' Lucky asked me.

"We both looked at the broken mowers; I looked at him and said, 'Let's go to break.'

"He thought I was the foreman and I thought he was the foreman. We called the rest of the workers and we all headed for a nearby store.

"'How much money do we have?' I asked everyone. We pulled our money together and bought some burritos. After the break, we walked back to the apartments.

"Just then, the foreman, who had dropped us off, arrived. 'OK, guys, let's go to lunch.' Lucky and I looked at each other. That's when we realized neither one of us, was the foreman!

"When we got back to the office the foreman was mad because the lawn mowers were broken. The machine maintenance repair guys accused us of breaking the already malfunctioning mowers. Before we knew it, one of the guys threw a punch a big fight broke out.

"Immediately, Lucky and I got back to back. 'I got you covered Frank!' Between both of us, we beat up the whole bunch.

Jerry Davey walked in and was disgusted at seeing the whole mess. He started cussing at everyone. After that fighting incident, Lucky and I became very good friends."

The Girl Who Prayed for Me

I had been working in the projects for about six months. One afternoon, Lucky and I were cleaning the trash that littered the projects and a little girl, about thirteen years old, roller-skated up to me. She stopped and looked up at me.

She said, "I prayed for you."

"Oh! Good, to get a better job?" I asked.

"'No!" She answered, "I prayed for you or somebody like you, to come and clean this place up. To throw out all the gang's, the sniffers and all those bad people. We can't play outside when the gangs come out. I'm just thirteen, and they grab me on my private parts and hold my buns real tight.

"Since you started working here and throwing them out, it's gotten better. I can roller-skate out here' ... She paused….. "But only when you're here. As soon as you leave, we stay in the house. That's why I prayed for you. I'm glad you're here. All of us kids are glad you are here."

I didn't expect to hear that. I realized there were over seventy-five kids who lived in the projects, and before I knew it, I got to be friends with all of them.

The kids learned to trust me and after a while, they weren't afraid to tell me who was responsible for the constant vandalism.

When I noticed things broken I asked, "Who broke that window?" And sure enough, they would point in the direction of the vandal.

During the time I worked for housing, I was offered really good jobs, but I didn't accept any of them. I could not leave those kids. I knew that if I left, things would get worse. So I stayed. I guess it was all in a day's work or months, actually years.

On the day that Jerry Davey swore me in as security, he had told me to get rid of all the troublemakers in the area. He also told me to help out any tenants who were trying to better themselves. And so I did. From the day he gave me those orders, I enforced them. If a particular tenant or any of their relatives living with them, kept acting badly, I served them an eviction notice and they were out in ten days.

The repairs on the units were never ending. Some tenants were afraid to let me into their houses to make the repairs.

I didn't blame them for being afraid. "Open the door please. I'm not here to hurt you. I'm here for you! Remember this, I belong to you, and you belong to me. I will not harm you!" I had to convince and reassure them that I was there to fix their homes and not abuse and take their money like the vandals did. My job was to make the projects safer for them and their children. It took a while for them to believe these words.

Lenora and I had been living in our apartment on West San Francisco & West Alameda city housing for a year. It had taken me that whole year to finally get rid of the gangs in these projects.

Without any notice, the housing moved us to a house on Gallegos Lane. It was a three bedroom and was also part of HUD housing. Jerry Davey wanted me to live there because the gangs were running the place and abusing the tenants.

That very first night we moved in, my kids went outside to play. It was late in the evening and a young guy about nineteen walked over to my yard and began harassing them. He had a dog with him and began taunting my dog with his.

The kids came running into the house to tell me what was happening, and then they ran outside again. I threw on my pants and went outside barefooted and without a shirt. Sure enough, the bully was cussing at the kids.

Figure 6 Frank Wiggins, HUD Housing, Gallegos Lane, Santa Fe, NM, 1982

Just then, he kicked my dog. "What the hell are you doing?" I yelled.

He came at me and threw a punch. Obviously, he didn't know who he was messing with. Before he could even release the punch, I hit him real hard several times. He landed on the ground with blood all over his face. Within minutes, I saw lights flashing and a cop car arrived on the scene.

"You can't hit that man like that!" the cop shouted.

"Yes I can!"

"No, you can't," the cop yelled back.

"Well then, get down and come help him," I threatened him.

"Back up is coming right now!" He shouted back. All the while, he didn't come out of his car. Several minutes passed and the cop called me over to his car, "Come over here! I want to talk to you."

When I approached, he repeated himself, "You can't hit anyone like that. What's your name?"

"Frank E. Wiggins," I answered.

He was talking over the CB radio, "The suspects name is Frank E. Wiggins." I heard sirens approaching in the distance.

Suddenly, a voice over the cop's radio came over loud, "Jimmy Melendrez! Get the hell out of there and let Wiggins do his job! RIGHT NOW! Get out of there!"

Jimmy looked at me. His eyes were real big. Then he turned his sirens on and took off real fast.

When I was still working just as a maintenance employee at the apartments, Jerry Davey tried to get me more help, but the only person who was not afraid to help me, was Lucky.

Lucky and I cleaned up the neighborhood, and that included the bad elements. At first, we fixed above thirty-five windows a day. Almost every window in the projects was broken or cracked. We fixed doors, repaired screen doors, and cleaned up all the yards. There were dirty diapers, trash, and sniff rags. The dumpsters were half-full of dirt, half full of trash. Lucky and I had to take the dirt out of the dumpsters.

During the first two months, we made four to five dump runs a day cleaning the filth from the projects. After so much abuse, the dumpsters were in bad shape. They were cracked and had broken wheels. I put in an order for new ones, and it was approved.

Lucky and I were a good team. If we caught people painting graffiti on the walls, we made them paint the walls. And if they didn't show up, I went personally and got them from their house.

"You have two choices, either come and paint, or go to jail for destroying government property. You better tell me right now which one it'll be." I never accepted "no" for an answer.

I had a young man about eighteen years old painting because he had put graffiti on a building.

His father walked up to me and said, "I don't want my son painting."

"Your son was painting graffiti on the walls and if you don't want him painting, then you have to paint for him. I really don't care which one it is. You either have to pay with money, with painting, or someone has to go to jail. You'll go to a federal court for destroying government property and probably do time in jail. And also pay a big fine... it's up to you."

The man looked at me. I could tell he was weighing his options. "Take care of my boy," and then he turned to his son and said, "And you, you better do a good job!" He planted his hand on his son's shoulder and told him, "Don't you ever embarrass me again!" Before his father left, he asked me, "How long is my son going to have to pay?"

"It should take about an hour. He still has to paint the wall on this side of the building." He seemed satisfied with my answer and left.

Every time I caught vandals, I put them to work fixing up their own messes, some of them were not very cooperative. I had to be vigilant 24 hours a day 7 days a week. Jerry Davey was getting complaints from some of the tenants about their "hijítos" getting hurt. I guess I left too many of them with broken bones.

One day Jerry called me into his office. "Frank, we're going to get sued!"

"Do you want me to stop?" I asked him.

He sat in his chair mumbling something or other and then said, "Go back to work."

I remember one time Lucky and I responded to a call about a fight. There was a bunch of guys at one of the projects drinking and disturbing the peace. They were waiting for me, and when I got there, a young man ran up to me with a gun and pointed it to the side of my head.

It all happened real fast. I heard a click as he pulled back the hammer, then right as he pulled the trigger, Lucky was there. In a split second Lucky jammed his thumb between the hammer and the gun case. Lucky began struggling with the man.

The young man had a good grip on the gun and was waving it over my head. I grabbed it and twisted the gun out of the guy's hand. Lucky had saved my life! He was like the eyes in back of my head. When we disarmed the young man, I was very angry. But Lucky, he was worse off than me. The Marine Corps had thrown him out of the military for being kill crazy. By the time Lucky was through with this guy, that young man was taught a big lesson.

The Camper

"Dad, tell me the story about the Camper."

"Oh yeah, I remember. There was never a dull moment in the projects, and almost every day was unique. One night about 11 o'clock, I was responding to a call from a tenant at one of my housing projects. I called them 'My' housing projects because I was in charge of four housing locations around the city, including four Senior Citizen Housing centers, eight locations in all.

"These particular projects were located just beyond Saint Francis Street. There was a Federal Bank on the corner and behind it was a dirt area surrounded by beautiful big trees which belonged to the projects too.

"As I was nearing the street to turn right toward the projects, I saw an RV camper parked in the vacant dirt area. Nobody ever parked there, but that wasn't the case this evening. I became suspicious when I noticed something hanging out of the closed RV door.

"I looked closely; it was a roll of beautiful red ribbon which had rolled out for about twenty-five feet from the camper. There was also a small piece of a blue ribbon hanging out from the closed camper door.

"I parked my truck, walked quietly to the camper, and knocked on the door. There was no answer. I walked back to my truck and got a bat from the bed. Again, I knocked on the door, but still there was no answer. I could hear noises from inside.

"I took a swing with my bat and broke the door knob off then slowly opened the door. I heard a noise coming from the floor, there was a man behind the driver's seat, tied up and gagged.

"Without warning, five young men darted from the rear of the RV. Before I could stop them, they ran over the table and escaped out the open door. One more guy followed behind, and he too sprinted out the camper with them.

"I rushed to the back bedroom. There were two beds, and on one of them, was a girl about thirteen years old. She lay naked with her hands and feet tied to the bed. On the other bed, was a woman tied up the same way, she was probably her mother.

"I ran back to the front to untie the father. Half way there, I heard a noise. There on the floor, off to one side; was a young boy. He too was tied up and his mouth gagged.

"I untied the man first. 'Go back there and check on your wife and your little girl.' I told him. He ran to the bedroom.

"Meanwhile, I untied the boy who was crying uncontrollably. In the end, everything was okay. Luckily, I got there before anything worse happened.

"When the woman and girl were dressed, the father asked me, 'Could you take my wife and daughter to the hospital?'

"They appeared to have bad scrapes and bruises, so I asked him, 'Do you want me to call an ambulance or police?'

"'No,' he quickly responded. 'I don't want anyone to know about this. Can you give me a ride?'

"'Yes, of course.' I answered.

"I couldn't fit all of them into my truck. The husband insisted I take his wife and the little girl first, and so I did. I came back for the man and his son.

"Before we left, the man tried to lock his camper door. I had broken the knob off, so he couldn't secure it. He was worried about leaving it unlocked in case someone else tried to vandalize it when they were gone. I went to my toolbox and got a padlock and hasp, a hinge to lock the padlock with.

"As I was screwing the hasp onto the door, the man asked, 'How did you know?'

"'How did I know what?' I answered.

"'You came back... when no one answered the door. How did you know?'

"'I suspected something was wrong when I saw the red and blue ribbons coming out of the closed RV camper door.'

"We got in the truck and I saw tears rolling down his cheeks.

"I asked, 'Did you get hurt real bad?'

"'No,' he answered.

"'Why are you crying?'

"'Today, I got mad at my little girl because she wasted money buying those ribbons. I took them from her and threw them out the door. I have money, but I wanted to teach her a lesson. About spending money on what I thought were frivolous things. Little did I know the damn ribbons were going to save our lives?'

"Tears continued to pour down his face. When we got to the hospital, I asked him, 'Do you need a ride back to your camper?'

"'No, thank you, I'll get a taxi or a ride somehow.' He repeated several times, 'Please, don't tell anybody! I'll take care of everything myself.'

"He thanked me again and gave me a big hug. 'Thank you, thank you! I'll pay you back somehow.'

"'No,' I told him. 'I can't take any money... I was just doing my job... I work with security for City Housing.'"

"Did you ever see the man again?" Ray asked.

"No, that's the last time I saw him. I never asked him his name either.

"Something very interesting happened the following week. It was the end of the day on Friday and I was driving back from the housing office. I parked the truck up close to my house, and in my rear view mirror, noticed something in the bed of the truck. I walked to the back. It was a case of Pabst Blue Ribbon beer, wrapped with a red ribbon.

"The following Friday, there was a bottle of Canadian Mist, wrapped in a blue ribbon. And the Friday after that, there was a bottle of Jack Daniel's, wrapped in red and blue ribbons. That was my favorite! It never failed. I got these small gifts every Friday for about a year. It only stopped when I moved to California, in 1982.

"It's been over 30 years since that incident. I really hope they're all alive and doing well."

"Dad… when you started working for the housing, did you know what you were in for?"

"I really didn't anticipate the enormous job that was ahead of me. I only started working with the housing out of necessity. Our family needed the basics for day to day living, and they depended on me. I knew that just receiving food stamps, was not enough.

"Through my experience of working at the housing, I got to help a lot of people, from the Governor to the poorest person in the projects. I tried to give meaning to their lives. I was not a person who could get bought off. I was offered money to ignore regulations on some jobs, but I never took it.

"I was happy with what I was doing. I knew that I was making a difference. I felt like I was giving freedom to people, that before, had no hope. I began to look at the projects as my own personal domain.

"I would tell my wife, 'I hate the way that people destroy my projects.' Her reply was, 'Well… Now you know how God feels, when he sees his earth being polluted and destroyed!'

"In the beginning, when I accepted the job as security for the Housing Projects, it wasn't for the money. There was no extra pay. At the time, Jerry Davey had told me the City Housing budget didn't have enough money for this position. But I took on the additional responsibility anyway. On the books, I worked for maintenance. Any additional time I put in for security, I could take time off if I wanted.

"I knew that eventually, I would leave the job, but, I just couldn't leave without making some improvements. There was so much work to be done, and I wasn't afraid to do it.

"Jerry had lots of confidence in me. Every year, right before Christmas, he asked us to submit a Christmas list of repair work. Work that we felt the projects really needed. I turned in my list. I requested a complete renovation of the projects, inside and out. My co-workers laughed, they made a bet my request would be denied because I was asking for too much.

"'It isn't for me! Dummies, it's for them! It's for the people.'

"If you had taken a ride through the projects five years later, you would have seen that my request was granted. Everything I asked for on the list was done.

"During the time I was employed there, I know I helped the elderly people regain some of their dignity. To this day, when I run into people who remember me, they can't stop being grateful. They wished I had stayed.

"The young adults, who were children at the time, are always happy to see me whenever I run into them in town. I can still feel their heartfelt gratitude as they greet me with a handshake and a hug. I made a difference in many people's lives.

"The projects were run by undesirables, drug abusers, snifters, and gangs. They were harming innocent people. They were taking the old people's social security money, molesting defenseless young people, beating up anyone they wanted, and destroying and damaging government property.

"As I mentioned earlier, I left the projects in 1982 and moved to California.

"Two years later, in 1984, I came back to Santa Fe to visit family. I also wanted to see some of the people in the projects.

"That same day, I found out there was some kind of celebration taking place at one of the housing locations. When I arrived, I mingled through the crowd. I heard the mayor and some other big wigs giving speeches and they were taking credit for all the positive changes in the projects.

"Rick Marez, and most of the crew from Housing, were there too. But even they, were not getting any credit.

"One of the housing tenants noticed me in the crowd. I heard him say, 'Hey, Frank Wiggins is here!'

"Heads started turning in my direction and pretty soon a bunch of people came to greet me. The Mayor noticed the commotion and wanted to know who I was. I saw Rick Marez telling the Mayor that I was the person who had changed the projects. And that I should be receiving the credit for these changes.

"Rick Marez finished talking to the Mayor and made his way to where I was at. 'Frank, the Mayor wants to know if you want to give a speech.'

"'No,' I said. It was already the end of the event and when he asked me if I wanted to give a speech, everybody was leaving. I noticed that as soon as Rick left the podium, the Mayor said the event was over. To this day, the city hasn't even thanked me for my contributions.

"I remember when we first moved into the projects, there was a sign on the wall that read:

Silver City
Enter at your own risk

Today the sign reads:

VILLA ALEGRE"
(Happy Village)

17

THE FLASHBACK

"Lost In Time"

I worked for the Santa Fe Housing Authority from 1978 to 1982, and quit when my boys graduated from high school. My boys were all one year apart in age and coincidentally, all four boys graduated from Santa Fe High School the same year. Two of the boys were a little behind from changing so many schools. One was on schedule and the other was ahead. Lenora and I had talked it over. We wanted the boys to find better jobs, but since there were very few in Santa Fe, we decided to move back to San Jose, California.

When we arrived in San Jose, we didn't have enough money to get our own place right away, so in the meantime, we lived with one of my nephews and his family in San Jose. The boys found jobs right away. Three were hired at a cabinet door company, and the other at a machine shop. We lived with my nephew for only 15 days. What luck, we found a house for rent just down the street from my nephew. The house needed lots of repairs, but the boys were old enough to fix everything.

At first, my sons didn't want me to get a job right away. "Take a break Dad... Try relaxing and go fishing!"

I laughed just remembering. I had a great time being with them. I couldn't remember the last time I was this happy. Every morning, we went to work together. I dropped all of them off at work and then came back to my house. I did this for about four months, and then that got old.

On this particular morning, I took the three boys to the cabinet door company, and then took Frankie Jr. to his work at the machine shop. I then went back to the cabinet door company and waited for the boss to arrive. I had noticed the boss always came in about nine o'clock and it was barely 8:30, so in the meantime, I went to their lunch room to wait.

I anticipated the boss to walk into the lunch room, but instead, the company owner entered. "Good morning," I greeted him, 'how are you doing today?'

The owner smiled. He knew who I was because he saw me leave my boys off every morning. "I see you stayed around to watch," he answered.

We talked for a while, basically about nothing. I was waiting for the right time to pop my question. "Are you hiring any drivers?" I asked him.

"Yeah, as a matter of fact, we need a driver to drive to Las Vegas. Let me talk to my son Ed, he runs the whole place."

"Do you want me to wait around?" I asked him.

"Yes, I'm going to the office right now.... wait here and I'll ask Ed right away."

I waited for about forty-five minutes. At 9 o'clock, all the workers came into the lunch room for their break. Everyone was very friendly.

One greeted me with, "Hello, how are you?"

Another asked, "Are you Ray's dad?" "Yes I am!" Then another said, "You got three boys working here, right?"

Just then, my boys walked in. "Hey dad! What are you doing back here?"

I joined them and we laughed through the entire break. When break was over, everyone went back to work.

At that very instant, Ed came into the lunchroom, he asked, "How are you doing, Frank?"

"I'm doing good thank you," I said. 'I was talking to your dad, and he says you may need a driver.'

Ed looked at me with a slight frown then asked, "Do you know how to drive a truck?"

"Yes."

"Do you have a California driver's license?"

"Yes I do!"

"Do you know the LA area?"

"Oh, yeah, I used to live there."

"Okay, we can pay you eight dollars an hour, how does that sound?"

"No, that's not enough."

"Okay.... how about ten dollars?"

I thought about the new offer then countered, "If I accept that, you have to pay me from the minute I leave to the time I get back."

"Okay," Ed replied. "Are you ready to go to work tomorrow morning?"

"Yes sir, I am."

I never had problems getting a job. I went home right away to tell my wife, Lenora, I was going to be working with the boys. I was also excited to have a job again.

The following morning I went to work with the boys. My truck was already loaded and ready to go and the boss handed me maps of Reno, Nevada. They gave me a GMC truck; actually, it was a big van. The shop called it the "million dollar truck," because of all the repairs they put into it just to keep it going. It ran really good for me, and I drove it all over Reno, Nevada, Los Angeles, and Arizona.

I worked for the Cabinet shop for about four or five months. All the while, I was putting away some of my earnings and when I had saved $3,000; I looked around for a truck to buy.

I found a Kensworth for $7,000 and put the $3,000 as a down then made arrangements to pay $500 a month for the remainder. The truck needed a lot of work, but in a matter of months, I restored it.

I left the cabinet door business and started my own trucking business hauling gravel and tomatoes. I didn't have a chauffeur license so I hired a young black man named Morris Bragg, to drive for me. During the rainy season, business slowed down so Morris did other things to make ends meet. I had no idea he committed robberies. Eventually, Morris got caught and was sentenced to prison. I was out of luck; now I was without a driver.

I had no choice but to get my chauffer license. Within two weeks, I had it. I taught my oldest son, Frankie Jr., to drive the truck, and he too, got his chauffer license.

I was earning $11,000 a month with that one truck. Again, I saved money and bought another truck, a Ford diesel. Frankie drove one truck and I drove the other. Our business was doing well. I bought a third truck and my other son, Willie, drove that one. I had the trucks hauling 24 hours a day seven days a week.

We had to hire more drivers. At one time, we were making $30,000 a month. My son, Louie, and my wife, Lenora, were doing all the dispatching. Even my youngest daughter, Jaime, helped out. Jaime was only in third grade but she was smart.

I was a sharp business man. When business began slowing down, I figured trucks always needed tires fixed and so I started a tire service. It was too expensive to advertise in the yellow pages of the telephone book, so instead, I bought an advertisement page in a trucking magazine. Man, did that work. We were making very good money with the trucking and the tire service business.

We ran the two businesses for about four years until the boys wanted out. They were tired of the business, and didn't want to do it anymore. I didn't want to do it without them, so I sold everything and we decided to move back to Santa Fe, New Mexico.

In September of 1988, Lenora, Jaime, and Ray moved to Santa Fe while Frankie, Louie, Willie, and I stayed to finish out some of our contracts. I had Ray drive Lenora to Santa Fe and move her into a double wide trailer we rented from my sister-in-law and her husband.

Then, in December of 1989, Frankie and I joined the rest of the family in Santa Fe. The only ones who stayed in California were my sons, Louie and Willie. To this day, Louie is the only one that still lives there.

"A month after I returned to Santa Fe, we moved into my niece's trailer house. My niece was getting a divorce, and so we took over her house payments."

"What year was that Dad?"

"It was 1990. I even remember the day we moved into the mobile trailer. It was August 15."

"And you're still here," Ray smiled.

"Anyway," I said to Ray, "Let's get back to the story, my memory is good today.

"When we first moved into the trailer park, I thought I was back in the projects. The neighborhood was unsafe. There were burglaries and vandalism."

Ray laughed; he remembered what I did to make it better.

"What can I say?' I grinned, "I cleaned up the graffiti and got rid of the thugs around the neighborhood.

"It was during this same time that a friend of mine, David, wanted me to partner with him in a landscaping and gardening business. I agreed, and invested some of the money I got from selling the trucks in California.

"I bought a rotor tiller, lawn mower, edger, blower, and shovels, basically everything. At first, we just had a small crew. We did landscaping, painting, and other side jobs. It was good money, but not as good as the trucking business I had had in California.

"David wanted to make more money so on the side; he sold hats, knives, and wallets at the flea market. I decided to do that too and soon, I too was making pretty good money. I was doing better than David.

"He became jealous and didn't want to work with me anymore. And so we went our separate ways, but not before he wanted his share of the tools.

"One day, he showed up and wanted to take half of the equipment and tools. 'Frank, I came to get my tools.'

"'Okay,' I told him. I jumped in the back of the truck and threw out a rake, pitchfork, and a few other small things.

"'That's all?' David questioned.

"'That's all, the rest is mine. I bought it with my money. The only other thing you put in was your business name.' He got mad and left.

206

"I continued with the business and had plenty of customers, but was short on help.

"Thanks to a nephew of mine, I found some workers. My nephew had done some time in prison and knew these guys who had just been released from the jail. They needed a job, and I needed reliable workers, which they were. I hired about twenty of them.

"Some of the guys were covered with tattoos. I wanted to maintain a respectable business so I made them cover their tattooed arms when they were on the job with me. I also didn't want my clients getting spooked.

"While in the landscaping business, I also started a tire service again. I named it "Coyote Trucking." That's when I began making some good money."

The Flashback

"One day, my nephew and I were visiting one of his friends, his name was Michael. It happened that Michael's father, Mike, was a veteran. Mike and I laughed and shared stories. He told me some funny stories about his military experience and I told him stories about my dare devil death wish escapades after leaving the military.

"Toward the end of our visit, Mike looked at me; the smile had disappeared from his face.

"He said, 'I'm going to give you something that you're going to need later, but not now, because you can't see it.'

"He gave me a pamphlet. It had information and the telephone number of the VA's Post Traumatic Stress Disorder

Program. Eight months later, I had one of the worst flashbacks of my life. That pamphlet, led me to the road I travel today."

"Tell me exactly what happened?" Ray asked.

He knew this was going to be hard on me. It didn't help that I couldn't remember things very clearly since the flashback.

"I remember it was a cloudy day and I was returning from Espanola. I had my tire service business and had gone to fix a tire. The business was doing well, we repaired semi-truck tires and there were a whole lot of trucks on the road. When I finished the job in Espanola, I got a call to go fix another tire at the bottom of "La Bajada," but I never made it there.

"I was on St. Francis Street going south and veered onto the freeway, I-25 south, towards Albuquerque. I saw the Cerrillos Road Exit sign, and that is when the flashback started. In years past, I had experienced flashbacks, but had no idea how strong this one was going to be."

"What do you think set it off?" Ray asked.

"I'm not sure, what I do remember, is that it was cold and cloudy. One time, when I had just returned to LA from the army, I was on my way home and crossing a freeway bridge. The day was gloomy, it was cold and cloudy, and I started to feel something coming on. I was having a flashback. I got lost. The next thing I remember, I was on Highway 101, heading towards San Diego. I had no idea how I got there."

"Do you think certain weather triggers a flashback?"

"Could be… during my missions, the weather was usually cold and cloudy."

"Interesting... I'm sorry," Ray said, "I didn't mean to get us off track. What happened after you felt the flashback coming on?"

"I didn't want to come to a complete stop on the freeway, so I was pressing on the brakes slowly, trying to avoid being hit from behind. I felt the flashback's intensity increasing. I remembered the Cerrillos Road Exit and headed in that direction. It was coming on strong, so strong that my vision was becoming blurred. I couldn't see anything in front of me. Since I couldn't see, I was trying to feel or hear as my tires reached the gridded ridges on the shoulder of the pavement. I felt like I was going too far, when actually, I was still on the freeway exit ramp.

"You don't know how relieved I was when I felt my truck tires on the dirt. I didn't slam on the brakes, but stopped as quickly as I could. I turned off the ignition and just stayed there, with both hands tightly gripping the steering wheel.

"Immediately, a flood of pictures, sounds and smells invaded my head. I was having flashbacks of my missions in Germany. No matter how hard I tried to regain focus, I couldn't come out of it. I don't know how long I was sitting there, when I heard a voice outside my window.

"A State Policeman had pulled over and walked up to my truck. I knew practically all the state police in the area and lucky for me, I knew this one.

"He came up to my window and asked, 'Frank, are you alright?'

"'Yes...I'm real tired and just had to stop and rest for a while. I just came from one job and I'm on the way to another.'

"I couldn't look him in the face. I didn't want to tell him that I was having a flashback. I sure didn't want to lose my license."

"How long were you there?" Ray asked.

"It was 10:00 AM before I realized where I was. Where I had been in my head, I really don't know. I was shaking. It felt as if I had just zoomed out of a time machine, out of my seventh mission. I had relived it all over again, and it was horrifying. It was just like when you rewind a tape recording, over and over again. The flashback lasted eight hours, from 2:00 am to 10:00 am and to this day, those eight hours are lost in my mind."

"What happened next?' Ray asked.

"I started my truck and went home right away. As soon as I got there, I took all the tools and the compressor out of the back of the truck. I went inside and told Lenora I didn't trust myself on the road anymore. I was ready to turn in my driver's license. I didn't want to harm anyone. That day I walked away from my tire service business, 'Coyote Tire Service.'

"Ray, you didn't want me to close the business. I remember telling you I couldn't handle that stress anymore. There was something wrong with me. I was afraid that if I kept the equipment, I was going to be too tempted to drive. I didn't want to have another flashback and kill someone on the road.

"I was sick. Every day after this, I kept having more flashbacks, every few hours, but they weren't intense like the big one. A couple of weeks passed when I remembered the phone number on the VA Brochure my nephew's friend's father had given me months earlier.

"I called the number and spoke to someone named Rose.

"She took down my address and said, 'I'm going to be sending you a packet with information for you to fill out. When you're done, bring the packet over to the Veteran's Hospital. Don't talk to anyone in your family about this. They might want to talk you out of it.'

"I filled out the papers and in a few weeks, drove myself to the Veterans Hospital in Albuquerque.

"As I mentioned before, in the past I had owned and operated several very successful businesses. First I had the trucking business and then the plating shop in San Jose. I walked away from the plating shop and left my brothers to run it, and I sold the Trucking business when my sons got tired of it.

"My sons were my right hand and I didn't want to continue running the business without them. I was making plenty of money with both businesses. Finding jobs and making businesses work was not a problem for me, but keeping them was."

18

A TIME FOR HEALING

"I Am Not Alone"

"All these years I knew something was wrong, but I didn't know it as an illness, a wound in the heart and mind that is not visible. The wound was so deep, that I used marijuana to self medicate and hard liquor to numb the pain and memories of what had taken place on that seventh mission.

"I went for help, but at first the VA could not process my papers. This was when they said my DD214 looked different than the newer ones and accused me of making it up. The VA also said my DD214 didn't say I was ever in Germany even though there was an APO number on the DD214. Every soldier knows that APO numbers are only given when a soldier goes overseas. The APO number proved that I was in Germany; it is like a zip code.

"To make matters worse, when I met with them again a few weeks later, they claimed my DD214 was lost.

"'Sorry, Mr. Wiggins, but we can't find your DD214, so we can't process your papers.' The guy went to his office and pretended to look for it again. He rummaged through a pile of papers on the desk then came back and shook his head, 'Sorry, it's not there.'

"'That's okay,' I told the intake clerk, 'I have another copy. It's a notarized copy of the original. I have it at home.' He seemed surprised."

"Dad, why did you have a copy made?'

213

"It just so happened that a few weeks earlier, while I was waiting for this appointment, I had talked to a VFW representative.

"He said, 'Frank, you should make a few notarized copies of your DD214, it's pretty old and that may be the only one in existence.' Lucky for me I took his advice."

"I had been to the VA hospital three times in the last two weeks. I was trying to qualify for veterans health benefits so I could get help. Finally, Doreen, one of the Drug & Alcohol Abuse Program counselors in Building 1, came to my rescue. She saw I was in bad shape.

"She said, 'Frank, while they make up their minds and look for your paper, I'm going to admit you to Ward Seven but, you have to be at your best behavior because they'll throw you out... Comprendė?' (Understand?)

"I laughed at her comment but assured her I would.

"Maggie, the other counselor in the program, stepped in, "I'll personally take responsibility for him!"

"I was relieved and thankful for these two counselors who were trying to help me.

"While I was in Ward Seven undergoing evaluation, I asked my wife Lenora to write a letter to the program. I knew there was something wrong with me. I needed help and wanted the doctors to hear it from my wife too.

"I had held so many jobs since my return from Germany. I couldn't stay in any one place longer than six months. My wife made a list of the numerous jobs I had had. She also made a list of the dozens of places we had lived. Lenora could only list by name forty of the hundreds of jobs she remembered.

"She listed at least 35 places we had moved to. I moved my family from city to city and state to state. Literally, from one end of a county to the other and back again. This is the letter she wrote:

TO WHOM IT MAY CONCERN: 6/2/95

Please let me begin by saying that I am very happy that my husband decided to get some help for his problems. I have often told him through the years he should get help for his problems, and his reply to me has been "I don't have any problems but you."

I understand that alcohol is a food substance and can turn into an addicting drug that can ruin many parts of your body organs. Marijuana, on the other hand, is an addicting chemical that can also be very damaging to a person's health and well being. It can remain in one's body, as well as the brain cells for a long time, perhaps through a person's life span depending on how often they use it.

My husband, I believe, has both these problems, which through the years have gotten progressively worse. He never wanted to admit that he was an alcoholic, he often said "I can quit whenever I want, if I were an alcoholic I couldn't do that." So he would quit for a few months to prove to his family that he wasn't an alcoholic. As for Marijuana he quit for a short time but made sure to tell me that he was not doing it for me!

Frank and I have been married 35 years. We got married two months after he got out of the Army. Soon after I got to see that he was a very restless kind of person. We never lived in one place too long; his employment record span was the same. Whenever he got the urge to move, we would move on the spur of the moment. He would quit his job if someone even looked at him cross-eyed. Even after our babies started coming, that didn't stop him from his sudden urge to move. If it wasn't from one city to another it was from one state to another; our children would always have to change schools. At first it was like an adventure it was real exciting and fun. In time it became drudgery, we were like gypsies, always on the move.

His drinking and drugs became unbearable through the years. Along with this was the mental anguish of having to cope with the

215

accusations and the fear he instilled in me, talking about guns and how much "fun" he had in the army and how his adrenalin would rise and how exciting it was to go after the enemy. He was very secretive about details concerning his duties. He would only talk about how much he loved doing it, whatever it was; I could only come to conclusions.

Sincerely,

Lenora G. Wiggins

Figure 7 - Letter from Lenora, my wife, to VA, June 2, 1995

"After a month in Ward Seven, I was transferred to Ward Five. It was also a drug abuse and anger management unit, but at least this Ward had a little more freedom."

"What's so funny Dad?" Ray asked.

"Oh, I was just remembering one of the interviews when I was in Ward Seven. I told the counselor the story about my car that got a lot of repairs I didn't ask for, and how they didn't want to give me my car back until I paid. No one died, but I took care of the guys who owned the garage."

"Yeah," Ray answered, "I remember you telling us that story."

"Well, after telling the counselors that story, they wrote down on my chart that I was 'homicidal,' not, 'suicidal.'

"While in Ward Five, I was also diagnosed with PTSD, and this qualified me to be considered for admittance into the VA's PTSD program.

"Since the big flashback, I had trouble focusing and concentrating. I use to have a photographic memory but now I tried to read and couldn't comprehend what I was reading. As the years go by, I don't even attempt to read anymore.

"'Mr. Wiggins,' the psychologist had told me, 'The reason you can't focus on things is that you have **Chronic PTSD**.'

"Dr. Evelyn Sandeen was in charge of the PTSD program at the VA and Doreen, my counselor, asked Dr. Sandeen if I could get into the program. I found out there were already about four or five other veterans also waiting to be accepted, so I didn't know what my chances for the program were. Then on June 30, 1995, Dr. Sandeen approved my eligibility for admittance.

"Originally, the program wanted to keep me in Ward Five as a residential patient, but the Ward was so full that they put me up at a nearby hotel. The VA fed me breakfast, lunch, and dinner.

"For nine months, I drove in from Santa Fe on a Sunday night, stayed in a hotel until Wednesday night, and the VA PTSD program paid for it.

"After each session, I walked over to my hotel room and did not go anywhere. Wayne and Andy, who were also in my PTSD group, always came to my hotel to take me out to eat. Andy didn't like me being all alone. He used to pick me up from the hotel and take me to run errands with him. Sometimes, he took me to his house in Taylor Ranch to visit a while.

"Most of the time I didn't remember very much because of all the medications the VA had me on. The drugs were very strong. It was like living in a cloud.

"On Thursdays, right after the program, I would go home to Santa Fe."

19

NEVER SO HUMILIATED

"I Am a Survivor"

"Most of the veterans, who were in the PTSD group, were advised to put in their claim for combat related PTSD disability compensation, and so I did. To be approved for a claim was very difficult, even if a veteran's service was documented in their service record book.

"My case was no different. One veteran in our group had served in Korea during the Korean War and he too had been denied. He was a POW for three years. He was one of the famous 'Tiger Survivors.' He had been in the Army and after being honorably discharged, he submitted his claim. The government denied his benefits."

"What was the reason?" Ray asked.

"The VA responded by saying they felt he had "**sat out the war,**" because he was a prisoner of war.

"The man was so angry he never dealt with the VA again, until twenty years later when he re-filed his claim. It took another ten years, and now, thirty years later, he was finally granted his benefits. Sadly, they only allowed ten years back pay when he should have gotten thirty years because that is when he submitted his initial claim.

"I was helped by a VFW (Veterans of Foreign Wars) officer, the first time that I applied for my benefits. At that time, there were representatives working out of a trailer located behind

Building 1 at the VA. The VFW officer sent my paper work to the regional office, but my claim for PTSD was denied.

"They stated there was lack of evidence on record to verify that I was ever in combat, or a situation that would have caused combat related trauma."

Ray shook his head in disgust. "Of course your missions were not documented, that's because you were involved in covert operations!"

"After I received the denial letter, Andy, my friend, took me to the downtown Albuquerque VA Regional Office on Gold Street. I filled out paper work to get an appeal process started. We returned several times and finally, two months later, the Regional Office informed me they were going to make me an appointment with a VA Traveling Judge.

"The purpose of this hearing was to give me the opportunity to speak directly to the Judge. I needed to prove to him what I had done in the military. The Adjudication Officer requested I submit any documentation to help support my claim.

"Dr. Evelyn Sandeen, my V.A. counselor, and Jerry Davey, my former employer with HUD Housing, wrote these letters on my behalf:

DEPARTMENT OF VETERANS AFFAIRS
Medical Center
2100 Ridgecrest Drive SE
Albuquerque NM 87108

A.T. Breen, Jr.
Adjudication Officer

In Reply Refer To:

Re: F.E. Wiggins
554-52-1460

11/19/97

Dear Mr. Breen:

This letter is written at the request of Mr. Wiggins, who has been a patient of mine at the PTSD/Trauma Clinic at the Albuquerque VAMC since July of 1996. He has recently received another denial from you for service-connection for PTSD, based on lack of verification of claimed stressors and also on lack of documentation of his having PTSD. Mr. Wiggins has been documented to have PTSD, severe and chronic, by several professionals, including myself, in our treatment program. In my extensive history with Mr. Wiggins, his account of his stressors has remained consistent and has been totally believable, in my professional opinion. He states that he was selected, along with other soldiers purposely pulled from different platoons and different battalions, to cross enemy lines in then-East Germany. He encountered several extremely stressful events during these missions, including crossing mine fields and finding that an explosive device he set had killed German children. Upon returning after that last event, he refused to cooperate any more with the missions, and began drinking heavily. He subsequently had a 35 year history of heavy drinking and drug use. This extensive substance abuse has dulled his memories for the names of those with whom he served. However, he has recently remembered four names of fellow soldiers who would have known of the secret missions: Richard Rodriguez, rank of corporal, from Texas; another Richard Rodriguez, rank of Private, from Puerto Rico; a Private Pitman; and a Private Grassic. All were in his same company, 7th Army, 75th Artillery Battalion, A Battery, during the period from 12/58 to 12/59. If Mr. Wiggins story is true, that he was pulled for a politically sensitive mission behind the Iron Curtain, certainly it would not be highlighted in usual Army documentation.

Mr. Wiggins has completed the intensive treatment program for PTSD here at AVAMC. He was a full participant in the program, and no hint of fabrication or exaggeration in his traumatic memories was detected by me or any other professional on our team.

Sincerely yours,

Evelyn Sandeen, Ph.D.
Psychologist, PTSD/Trauma Clinic 116G

Figure 8 - Letter to the Board of Veterans' Appeals from Dr. Evelyn Sandeen

221

November 12, 1997

RE: Frank Wiggins
Santa Fe, NM 87501

To Whom It may Concern:

This document is being prepared by Jerry E. Davey (Retired) Executive Director of the Housing authority of the City of Santa Fe, NM in regards to a Former Employee (Frank Wiggins).

Mr Frank Wiggins was employed by The Authority during the years of 1978 & 1982 as a Maintenance/Security person. As Mr Wiggins lived on the project area he was quite familiar with the tenants that occupied the units at the site and the problems that existed. The authority's budget was very limited during these years and Mr Wiggins was very instrumental in over seeing this area. The site was infested with all types of gang related activities, i.e.... Drugs, prostitution, thievery, stolen goods etc...

Mr Wiggins at great risk to himself and his family, in a very short period of time helped to clean up the area of many of the bad elements mentioned above, by identifying the persons responsible for the activities, in order for the Authority to legally evict these persons from the site.

Mr Wiggins was involved on two separate Authority Housing Sites during his employment with the Authority in the process of eliminating criminal activities for the Authority.

Jerry E. Davey (Retired)

Figure 9 - Letter to VA Appeals Process by Jerry Davey

222

November 8, 1997

To whom it may concern:

I Marcos Herrera, was Frank wiggins' partner, from 1979 through 1982. During that time period, we were employed by the Santa Fe City Housing Authority, under the direction of Jerry Davey, Executive Director.

Frank and I served as maintenance and security, although, the latter was done mostly on our own recognizance. At that time, Frank and myself got rid of excessive amount of gangs and the criminal elements. The major part of our efforts were done after 5:00 p.m. We were not paid for those after hour jobs, however, we were both veterans, and we took it upon ourselves to wage war on the extensive burdens the people were under. The criminal environment was so bad at that time that the City Police would not enter the vicinity after dark.

In time, Frank and I were able to eliminate most of the gang violence, criminal activities and the destruction of housing unites in our assigned area. In turn, attained funding with the help of the Executive Director, Jerry Davey, to completely remodel all housing unites assigned to us.

I Marcos Herrera am still an employee at the Santa Fe City Housing Authority. It took about six years to accomplish the clearing of the criminal element, and to this day, the dangerous condition have not returned.

Sincerely

Marcos Herrera

Figure 10 - Letter to VA Appeals Process by Marcos Herrera

223

"During the time I was awaiting my hearing date with the traveling judge, I had another flashback.

"I had gone to the VA for an appointment. My friend Andy also had an appointment that day. Afterwards, we got together and I followed him in my car to his house in Taylor Ranch. Andy was very happy; finally, he had received his very first pension check.

"We went to Duncan Doughnuts and celebrated. It was late in the evening, must have been about 7:00 PM, and I needed to get back to Santa Fe. As I was leaving, Andy walked out with me and offered me some money. He knew my wife and I barely made ends meet every month because I couldn't work.

"'No, I don't need no money, I'm just going home,' I told him. Being the kind of person he is, he stuck the money in my shirt pocket. We got to talking and I forgot about it.

"As I was leaving, Andy shouted, 'Be careful, big brother. It's going to be raining very hard later... here and in Santa Fe. It looks like we're going to be getting a big storm.'

"So I left, and sure enough, it started raining really hard. I was driving slowly behind a Rig then he turned off and I kept going. It was raining very hard and suddenly I felt a flashback coming on. I was lost in time.

"I didn't know where I was and when finally I was able to focus, I saw a sign up ahead that read, "Las Vegas."

"I looked down at my gas gauge and it read EMPTY so I quickly exited and saw a gas station to my right. I didn't have any money and didn't know what I was going to do for gas. I was in a difficult situation.

"I thought, 'Maybe the guy at the gas station would be willing to trade some gas for my tool box.'

"I walked into the gas station and happened to stick my hand in my shirt pocket. I was shocked; I pulled out three one-hundred dollar bills. At that very moment, I remembered Andy had put some money in my pocket.

"The clerk saw me take out these big bills and said, 'You better not be showing that kind of money around here.'

"That night, instead of going 59 miles to my house, I traveled nearly 200 miles to get home.

"I have always been a good driver, but the heavy rain triggered a flashback that sent me into timeless space. I missed all the Santa Fe exits and everything in between. I went all the way to Las Vegas, New Mexico before realizing where I was.

"A few months went by before I received a letter in the mail informing me of the appointed time with the traveling judge. The letter included other formalities such as how I should present myself at the hearing. I remember specifically that it said to dress casual.

"I invited my wife Lenora, my daughter Vivian, and my two veteran friends, Andy and Jesus, to go with me.

"As we walked in through the front doors of the Regional Office on Gold Street, I wasn't expecting such a thorough security check. Even though I had chronic PTSD and was heavily medicated, I was hyper vigilant of my surroundings. I could not shake the elements of the intensive training I had received in the military. Day in and day out; I could not be any other way.

"Entering the security gate I had to empty all my pockets then security proceeded to scan a metal detector wand over my whole body.

"'Do you have any weapons on you?' asked the security guard.

"I answered without really thinking of any repercussions, 'I don't have any weapons on me but everything around me is a weapon… even your badge.'

"'Yeah?' questioned the guard, 'and how is that a weapon?'

"'I'll tear it off you and use that pin on the badge to take your eyes out.' I then pointed at a small desk with a spiked paper holder facing up and said, 'Even this right here, I'll grab it with my hand and punch you in the head with the spike.'

"The guard looked at me suspiciously. He quickly picked up the paper holder and took it over to another table across the lobby. The guard then motioned for me to move on.

"We all got into the elevator and went up to the third floor to look for the VFW office.

"An officer stood at the entrance to one of the offices, and directed us down the hallway to the courtroom. As we entered the make shift courtroom, I immediately scanned the area. It was not what I expected of a courtroom. There was a long foldout table with foldout chairs.

"I thought to myself, 'So this is how the government spends millions of our taxpayer dollars.'

"My attorney, the man from the VFW, sat down first. I sat to his left and my wife sat next to me. Next to my wife sat my daughter, Vivian, then Andy and Jesus. We were all facing forward when the judge came in.

"He walked out and stood directly across the table from me. He wore a nice white suit. It looked expensive.

"'Frank Wiggins,' he said, and scanned the room from right to left to see who was going to answer.

"'I am Frank Wiggins… Frank E. Wiggins.'

"The Judge looked at me, starting from my head down to my waist. The table was in the way or else he would have looked all the way down to my feet.

"'Did you know you were coming to court Mr. Wiggins,' the Judge asked.

"'Yes,' I answered.

"'Then why are you dressed like that?'

"To that I replied, 'The letter I received said to dress casual.'

"I remember thinking, 'You are not dressed casual, sitting there in a thousand dollar suit!'

"The Judge sat down and began the questions. 'You were discharged on an honorable discharge?'

"'Yes,' I answered and continued, 'You, the government, discharged me from Fort Dix, New Jersey, with only one month's pay. My DD214 says one lump sum which was $90 dollars. You took $10 dollars away for something that I didn't turn in back in Germany. So, I only had $80 dollars to come home with. The military was supposed to bring me back to Fort Ord or Oakland, California, but they left me in New Jersey.'

"The Judge seemed annoyed. He began to ask me a lot of questions about when I was discharged. And other questions that I thought were meaningless. His questioning reminded me of the way I was treated when I was discharged.

"I began to get a horrific headache. I started to lapse into flashbacks and a ringing sound echoed in my ears. Everything became muffled, I felt like there was cotton in my brain. I heard the judge's voice, but couldn't distinguish anything he was saying. I was observing everyone's eyes and they were focused on the judge as he asked me questions.

"The only time my VFW attorney said anything on my behalf, was when the judge asked me, 'How do you know you have PTSD?'

"Right away my attorney intervened, 'You can't ask him that question, we already know, and we have already established that he has PTSD.'

"The judge squirmed restlessly in his chair; it seemed to me he was trying to think of what else to ask. 'How long were you in the Army?'

"'I enlisted for three years,' I replied, 'And served only one year, 11 months, and 11 days. I quit because I was not going to kill anymore for them.'

"The judge continued to ask other questions, but I don't remember whether they were important or not. All I remember was that I was so angry.

"When it was all over, we left the building. I had never felt so humiliated in my life, and was still so very angry that I didn't want to talk much to anyone.

"It was well over a month when I got a letter from the VA saying that I had a docket date to go to court in Washington, D.C. in order to appeal my case.

"When I contacted my VFW attorney, he said I had to go to Washington, D.C. by myself for the appeal. 'Frank? You also have to pay your own way over there and back.'

"'That's impossible!' I told him. 'I have no money and I am not going by myself. You just want me to get killed and then it will be all over!' I was extremely upset. 'Thank you, but no thanks!'

"My attorney attempted to clam me down, 'Well, Frank, you have 30 days to let me know what you are going to do. If you don't put in for that court date within the 30 days, and later change your mind, then you will have to file again, and the process will start all over from the beginning. And if you get any back pay, it will be from the day that you reapply.'

"I did not want to be humiliated like that again in my life. I never stood back in that courtroom or go to Washington D.C. given those restricted conditions. I've gone through enough; my wife, my six kids and even my grandchildren; they have all been affected by my trauma.

"Many times I tried to write my story, but the people I relied on to write it, for various reasons, did not or could not follow through. My wife and children have attempted to help me too. They remember many of these events.

"Throughout my working career, I walked away from many jobs and consequently moved my family frequently. I believe they, too, have PTSD from my reckless behavior.

"One year ago, I was put on high blood pressure pills and the medication had a very interesting side effect, I could sleep at night and the nightmares began to fade. I couldn't believe it, I felt as if a cloud was lifted.

"I remember that about a month after I had started this medication, I got a call from my friend Andy in Albuquerque. I answered the phone, 'Hello, statue?' (Jokingly meaning, is that you?). We then laughed, as we always do, when he or I call each other.

"'How are you doing today, bro?' Andy asked.

"'I feel like spring time! You know how it feels when spring finally comes… That's how I feel. And that's how I've been feeling since I started this new medicine. It's given for high blood pressure, but one of the documented side effects, is that it helps with PTSD nightmares too. It really feels like spring! I can sleep Andy, I can sleep.' I was so happy.

"I took this medication every day until January 11th, 2010, that's when the VA had a mix up about my refill.

"The VA hospital is always changing our primary providers, residents, PA's (Physician Assistants), and other providers. There was some confusion about refilling my prescription and I didn't get my medication until January 23rd.

"During that time I experienced several flashbacks, including one where I was looking for my rifle and ammo.

"It hasn't been the same since I received the new refill. Because of the VA mix up, I went too many days without the medication.

Now, I'm not sure when the feeling of spring time will return for me..."

Figure 11 - Frank Wiggins, 2010

Appendix A

(This is a poem my son, Louie, wrote about me)

Harden Man of War and Family

Firm, Strict, harden man of war and family
Sweet home wayward child
Driven never for right or wrong
Proud man of good, nor bad
Firm, Strict, harden man of war and family
Sweet bitter love of life, living.
Invented trust behind barricades
Able bodied man in ditches
Running to and fro through deserts
Trails of trials left behind
Shake the dust of ridicule
Casualties of hated men and
Back yard wars will come again
Firm, Strict, harden man of war and family
Clear the house, Clear the housing
Clear the corridors of midnight creatures and moonlit crawlers
Feel the beat of your baton
Growl at the dogs and howl at the wolves
Blackened flesh and iridescent bones
The iron teeth of man's best friend
Firm, Strict, harden man of war and family
Speak a word, never love the man
Hate the world and love the moon
Lime and sand could marble heart in a concrete chest
Touch the fire and feel the fury of his breast
You harden man of war and family what now
Will your seed not fear the rogue warrior?
Strayed from his course, his battle
His field, his battlefield
And will your sapling be uprooted from the nurturing hand earth's care
Left to grow
Become towering trees that reach the heavens and produce fruitage
Without water

By Louie Wiggins (my son)

231

Appendix B – Photos

**Frank Wiggins and Cynthia Martinez (the girl who prayed for me)
32 years later**

**Frank E. Wiggins and Sons Trucking Company & Tire Service
1986, San Jose, CA**

PTSD RESOURCES

U.S. Department of Veterans Affairs (VA)
1-800-827-1000
http://www.va.gov

Disables American Veterans National Service Program (DAV)
877-I AM A Vet (877-426-2838) or (859) 441-7300
http://www.dav.org

Department of Veterans Affairs (VA) Vet Center Program
Vet Center Combat Call Center
877-WAR-VETS
http://www.vetcenter.va.gov/

Vietnam Veterans of America
1-800-VVA-1316
http://www.vva.org/

U.S. Department of Veterans Affairs
Center for Women Veterans
http://www.va.gov/womenvet/

Paralyzed Veterans of America (PAV)
PVA National Headquarters
1-800-424-8200
http://www.pva.org

National Veterans Wellness Center of Angel Fire, Inc
http://www.veteranswellnessandhealing.org

Acupuncturists Without Borders: Military Stress Reduction Project
http://www.acuwithoutborders.org/veteransprogram.php

ABOUT THE AUTHORS

FRANK E. WIGGINS

Frank Wiggins is a Cold War era veteran who has suffered from PTSD since his separation from the military in 1960. He considers himself very lucky to have survived many years of a destructive lifestyle. Since a young age, he discovered he had a photographic memory, and in the military, he became an exceptionally well trained soldier.

Frank is now in his seventies and resides in New Mexico. His story is unique, but at the same time, mirrors the story of so many veterans who suffer from PTSD.

In spite of everything, Frank possesses a great sense of humor and is driven by a desire to help other veterans with PTSD tell their story; he feels this is necessary for their healing.

ETTA CAVALIER, M.A., GCDF

Etta Cavalier is the coauthor and editor of "Seven Steps to Hell and Back." She is a counselor, educator, and artist.

Etta is married to a veteran who also suffers from PTSD. Her husband and Frank Wiggins met at a year-long PTSD Treatment Program in 1995 and their friendship has become one of brothers. It was through this association that Etta became involved in writing this book.

.